Healing the Dysfunctional Church Family

Healing the Dysfunctional Church Family

DAVID MAINS

VICTOR BOOKS®

A DIVISION OF SCRIPTURE PRESS PUBLICATIONS INC.
USA CANADA ENGLAND

Copyediting: Barbara Williams
Cover Design: Scott Rattray
Cover Illustration: Robert Bergin

Library of Congress Cataloging-in-Publication Data

Mains, David.
   Healing the dysfunctional church family / by David Mains.
      p.   cm.
   Includes bibliographical references.
   ISBN 0-89693-050-5
   1. Church work with problem families 2. Family—Religious life.
   3. Christian life—1960—   I. Title.
   BV4438.5.M36 1992
   248.4—dc20   91-37704
                                                                CIP

   4   5   6   7   8   9   10   Printing/Year   96   95   94   93   92

CONTENTS

Dedicated to
Douglas and Melissa Timberlake
and to all in the new generation
who love the church enough
to help her rediscover wholeness.

INTRODUCTION

If I'd had my way, I probably would have gotten out of attending the meeting. It was scheduled for Tuesday, right in the middle of my workday, and I knew it would take a while just to drive to the college where the lecture was being given. On top of that, the topic sounded to me like a real "downer"— Traits of Dysfunctional Families. But I had promised a friend I'd go with him.

When I arrived on campus with a couple of minutes to spare, he was waiting for me. We said our "hellos" and then walked directly into a crowded auditorium. Fortunately we found two seats together about halfway from the front.

The speaker was introduced almost as soon as we sat down, but I really wasn't all that attentive. My mind was still back in the office with my unfinished work. The applause ended and she began . . .

"For the next hour I need you to go back in your thinking to the place where you grew up. What town comes to your mind? How about a house? Can you remember the address? Where did you go to school at that time? Do you recall the car your family had? How many people lived with you?"

You know, it's hard to ignore questions like that even when you're trying to. Soon I found my thoughts traveling back in time some forty years, looking in on scenes I had all but forgotten.

The lecturer continued. "This hour I want to show you ways families can be dysfunctional. Maybe your family was that way, or partially so. I'll also tell you what a healthy family looks like. Hopefully, you'll be able to evaluate your growing-up experience. That's important because dysfunctions are often passed on from one generation to another, and the cycle won't be broken if you don't know what's healthy and what isn't!

"For example, if you were raised in a dysfunctional family, a family that didn't work the way it should have, love had to be earned. If you consistently got good grades, you were loved. But come home with a couple of low marks on your report card, and suddenly you weren't as loved as you thought you were. Any of you remember what that was like?

"You were loved if you scored the winning touchdown, but not if you missed the tackle . . . if in the orchestra you were first chair violin, but not if you played third chair.

"Hear me," the speaker continued. "In a healthy family you should have sensed your parents' love regardless of what you did. Your dad should have said, 'So you lost the election, honey; what difference does that make? You gave it your best shot. As far as I'm concerned you're still the most marvelous daughter a father ever had.' Or, 'Listen, son, you could have forgotten every line in the play and I still would have been proud of you.' See, in a healthy family love isn't given or withheld on the basis of performance. So what was your family like?"

By now the pile of work on my desk back at the office was all but forgotten. I was caught up with this new topic.

The lecture continued. "There's a certain amount of denial and delusion that goes on in a dysfunctional setting. Possibly your mother used manipulation to control the family. When there was tension she always got a terrible migraine so there was no way to talk problems through. When she got better, the subject didn't come up again because it might trigger another headache. 'Can't you just do what I say?' she implored. 'Don't make me suffer this way!' No one ever suggested that Mom needed a cure for more than a headache.

"Maybe your father was an alcoholic. But that reality was too painful for your family to deal with. Dad's drinking problem was never discussed, much less confronted. Denial and delusion. 'Sometimes Daddy likes to sleep on the front porch,' you were told. The truth was, he had come home drunk at 2 in the morning and Mom wouldn't let him in.

"In contrast, a healthy family is characterized by truth and honesty about problems like workaholism or an uncontrolled temper. Looking back, would you characterize your family as healthy or unhealthy in this regard?"

In all, fifteen traits of dysfunctional families were dealt with in that hour. "Unhealthy families are perfectionistic. In healthy situations the members are given freedom to make mistakes.

"Dysfunctional families communicate double messages. 'Show respect for everyone, but blacks — or Jews — or whoever — is different.' Consistent messages mark healthy families.

"Dysfunctional families are unable to have a good time together, to play. Laughter and spontaneity mark healthy families. What was it like in the family in which you grew up?" the leader would ask with each new point.

"Few homes are dysfunctional in every area," she said. "On the other hand, some 'model families' may be more dysfunctional than you might think.

"Now here's something important," the speaker continued: "To admit past dysfunction doesn't mean you think your parents were failures. They probably did as well as they were able. Quite possibly, the families in which your parents were raised were dysfunctional in some of the same ways that your family was. So you're not blaming your parents for what happened. You're just learning to recognize dysfunctional patterns and how they have affected you. This way you can make corrections and see some progress in your life."

Back at the office I set my work aside and again went through the list of unhealthy family traits. Then it dawned on me that the church family can often be marked by the same dysfunctions. For example, too frequently in the church love has to be earned.

In the family of God we frequently don't allow for mistakes. Though we know we're all sinners, we still hold to the illusion of instant sanctification. We pretend no one in the church has a problem with greed, or lust, or a nasty tongue, or manipulation, or alcohol.

As in unhealthy families, in the church we can give double messages. "Reach out to your unsaved friends, but be careful not to get too close to the unconverted." "Christians should be filled with joy—but be careful how that joy is expressed in a service."

I'm not blaming anyone. I'm just pointing out that recognizing dysfunctional traits in a church family can be a beginning step toward finding wholeness. If we don't deal with our problems, the church may be issuing certain people a *double* dose of trouble. They could be members of *two* dysfunctional families—their individual family, and the family of God. And it's really sad when the church is unhealthy, because we know it should be the best family in the whole world.

Again, recognizing dysfunctional traits in a church family is a beginning step toward finding wholeness. That's what this book is about. It won't cover all the dysfunctions I heard discussed that day at the college. I only intend to pick eight of the traits. This book won't focus on your family's past either. My point of concentration will be the present-day church. In this best-of-all families, what's healthy and what isn't? We don't want to assume something is normal just because we've gotten used to it. People can function in all kinds of families. Individuals develop ingenious coping mechanisms, but there's always a long-range price, and it would be nice for us not to have to pay it.

In some ways you could say that lecture I attended was disturbing. Don't misunderstand: I've always been grateful for the family into which God allowed me to be born. But like all families, it wasn't perfect. Now I'm able to see ways I've been perpetuating flaws I inherited.

But I'm no longer a child. I'm an adult. For the good of future generations, I can make changes. My family can know a greater degree of wholeness. Didn't my dear parents want that for their three children? Dad and Mom weren't able to go to college, but they sure made it possible for us to go. I'm positive it wasn't easy for them to pay our tuition.

So too, I can attempt to see to it that life is better for my four children—that their generation moves toward greater wholeness.

And the same principle holds true for the family of God. Yes, this topic could be disturbing. It may require some tough thinking. But with God's help, it could also result in the church taking steps toward wholeness in Christ.

I mean, your church isn't perfect yet, is it?

I didn't think so!

In the Book of Ephesians, the Apostle Paul writes about the church becoming "mature, attaining to the whole measure of the fullness of Christ ... growing up into Him who is the Head, that is Christ" (4:13). Now there's perfection!

CHAPTER ONE

LOVE THAT HAS TO BE EARNED

THE FAMILY DOGHOUSE

● Back when you were growing up, was there a doghouse in your family? Not outside for Fido, but a figurative doghouse that one of the family members always occupied?

Maybe there was a favorite child, another who was usually in a more neutral spot, but also a son or daughter everyone knew was regularly in the doghouse. That was for doing something bad or embarrassing. Along with putting a family member in that position went the withholding of love. For example, a parent might not talk to the person for days . . . or weeks . . . or months! The family "doghouse" can be an awful place for the person in it.

But how does one get relegated to the "family doghouse"?

Lots of ways. Maybe you didn't keep your room clean, or you broke something, or you stepped on the neighbor's flowers retrieving your Frisbee, or you wore your hair too long, or you dated somebody your parents didn't approve of, or one year you didn't drive home for Thanksgiving to be with the family. You can still be put into the family doghouse long after you leave the home in which you were raised.

Just as there would be a lot of hurt involved in having to live outside in a literal doghouse, so this position of receiving criticism is an awful place to be consigned to. You know that if you've ever been in it. That's why families tend to joke about who's in the "doghouse." The pain is too great to talk about in a more serious way.

A family doghouse is often part of a dysfunctional home where love is given more on the basis of performance than it is unconditionally. The unstated rule is, "Please me, and you'll earn my love. Go contrary to my expectations, however, and you'll know my displeasure, believe me!"

I remember a chilling conversation with an older man whose only son had been a great disappointment to him through the years. I don't recall ever hearing him say a kind word about this son. One day as we were talking the subject came up again. Out of curiosity I asked, "Do you still have any tender feelings or good memories about Pete?"

The older man's response was that years ago he had turned those emotions off to protect himself. "I have no feelings for him now at all," was what he said. "The way my son acted, I couldn't afford to. He was always a rebel. I believe if I heard that he died, it wouldn't affect me *that* much.

I recall thinking, *I'm so glad this man wasn't my father!*

Don't misunderstand. I'm not excusing the sins of this son. I'm just saying that regardless of what I did as a son—and believe me, I've done my share of foolish things—it comforts me to know that my dad loves me. Like the marvelous father in Christ's Parable of the Prodigal, my dad would still come running to greet me, arms extended in welcome, his body language saying, "Oh, David, my favorite second son, I'm so glad to see you!"

Not, "Oh, it's you again!"

I hope my wife, Karen, and I never make any of our four children experience the pain of feeling unloved just because they don't perform up to our expectations. They're far from perfect, but certainly none of them has ever been deserving of "doghouse" treatment.

THE CHURCH DOGHOUSE

I also pray that in the family of God we never make our brothers and sisters in the Lord, spiritual sons and daughters, experience the pain of feeling unloved just because they don't perform up to our expectations. If there's anything that should characterize the family of God, it is unconditional love—the kind of love our Heavenly Father extends our way.

In Ephesians 5:1 the Apostle Paul refers to us as "dearly loved children" of God. That's a great phrase. It has all kinds of warm overtones, doesn't it? Dearly loved children. "Be imitators of God, therefore, as dearly loved children and live a life of love, just as Christ loved us and gave Himself up for us" (vv. 1-2). In the previous verse Paul instructs all in the church to "be kind and compassionate to one another, forgiving each other, just as in Christ God forgave you" (4:32).

A word of clarification: The fact that God loves us unconditionally doesn't mean He excuses our wrongdoing. But be aware that while He calls us to walk His better way, He doesn't stop loving us when we stumble or fall.

Because God loves us unconditionally, we can extend the same kind of love to our church family. We can say to others, "I accept you and love you for who you are. You don't have to conform to my standards. But in this family we also want Christ to teach us to become more like Him. We encourage each other in this regard . . . sometimes with tough love, love that confronts . . . but that's still love. In this special family love is never withheld. At least, it's not supposed to be."

When driving around town have you ever seen a church with a doghouse behind it? Of course you haven't! So that settles it, right?

Not really, because we all know that as awful as it is to withhold love from someone in the spiritual family bearing Christ's name, that still happens!

For what reason? I grant you these will appear like stupid reasons when I list them, but I'll let you know what some of them are:

- Someone's taste in music is different.
- Someone wears clothes others don't think are appropriate for the Sunday morning service.
- Someone's been going to a charismatic Bible study.

- Someone's been going to a theater.
- Someone just has a peculiar personality. You know what I mean, don't you now?
- Someone talks too freely about her faith, witnesses more aggressively than what normal folk like us are comfortable being around.
- Someone's preaching style doesn't follow the accepted style of verse-by-verse exposition.
- Someone hasn't gone on the 50-Day Spiritual Adventure with the rest of us.
- Someone smokes.
- Someone breaks an unwritten code and dates a non-Christian.
- Someone prefers the *King James* rather than the *New International Version.*
- Someone fills a role in the church and does it poorly.

For one of those type of reasons, someone in God's family gets stuck in the proverbial doghouse. And that someone has to feel some pain before we'll let him or her back into the mainstream church life. Maybe we never will.

Sometimes, because of who you are, how God made you, or where you are in your spiritual pilgrimage, it's impossible to conform to the expectations of others.

Wouldn't it be great if you didn't have to?

If the people of God loved you anyway?

If they said, "We wouldn't for anything in the world have you experience the terrible pain of being cut off from the main body. Yes, we want you to become more and more Christlike. But God hasn't assigned us the task of crucifying you. That's not what it means for you to take up your cross!" Instead:

Love protects.
Love hopes for the best.
Love is kind.
Love trusts.
Love doesn't keep a record of wrongs.
Love isn't rude.

That's Paul writing to the church in Corinth in 1 Corinthians 13. In our day he might have written, "Love isn't given on the basis of performance. It shouldn't have to be earned."

CHRISTLIKE LOVE

I made a list of individuals toward whom I have trouble extending Christlike love. It surprised me to see the number of names I came up with.

If I'm not careful my attitude toward these people is, *If you want me to be nice to you, you're going to have to earn it ... and that means you'll have to change your ways!*

My list has seven categories. See if you can identify with any of my struggles.

1. People whose needs seem never-ending. I prefer helping those who, before too long, can make it on their own. I start getting impatient when someone's problems are a continual drain on my bank of time or money or Christian love. I'm not defending my attitude; I'm just trying to be honest. Going the second mile with needy folk comes easy for me, but not running twenty-six-mile helping-marathons back to back! Unfortunately, a lot of people today need more than fast help every now and then.

2. Those people I do a lot for, but who don't seem to be very appreciative. These are individuals who take what I give and hardly say thanks. They act as though I owed them my help. Or they're people who almost resent what they see as my supposed advantages over theirs, and never notice what the relationship costs me. That's when I start thinking, *Before I extend you any more kindness, you're going to have to earn it!*

3. Individuals I sense are out to get me. I really have trouble loving those people. Maybe I said something honest and straightforward—it might have been in a sermon, even a word from the Lord—and apparently it stung. This man (or woman) took a general challenge and personalized it. Resentful, he subsequently used his influence to undermine me or my ministry—saw to it that certain doors never opened to me. It's not to my credit, but I find this kind of treatment hard to swallow. In such circumstances, for me, it's not easy to be Christlike and to keep extending love.

4. *People I don't feel I can trust.* They say all the right words—I just don't believe them. Like the consummate politician, they're great at talking out of both sides of their mouth. Characters like this can be discovered in novels and movies and television shows, but I find they pop up every so often in real life as well.

5. *Those who are incredibly slow at realizing they've disappointed me.* They're naive, surprised by my feelings. "I just didn't understand," they respond. "If I had known, I would have been far more sensitive, believe me. It just never dawned on me that you were going through so much pain."

6. *Individuals who haven't been loyal.* Especially when they make a big thing about being on my side. "When push comes to shove, I'm in your corner, brother." But when I need this person, I turn around and he's nowhere in sight. When that happens I get mad—say things I shouldn't.

7. *People who shut me out of their world.* There's something about me, I'm not sure what it is—how I act, what I believe, the things I say—that makes some people cautious: "Be nice, but keep Mains at arm's length. Don't ever let him on the inside!" Usually I'm not quick to pick up that this is happening. It takes me awhile to realize what's going on. But when I finally do figure it out, my UNCHRISTIAN response is, "Forget you, pal. I'll just exclude you from my world too."

CHRIST'S EXAMPLE
Christ also knew individuals like the people I've just described. He met those whose needs seemed never-ending, impoverished folk, the solve-one-problem-and-another-surfaces kinds of people. And there were those Jesus did a lot for, who didn't seem very appreciative—like the nine healed of leprosy who never said thanks. Only the tenth came back and expressed gratitude to Christ. Jesus encountered people out to get Him, to trick Him, to trap Him, to accuse Him, to kill Him—people He knew He couldn't trust. Others were incredibly slow at understanding what Jesus' ministry was all about. The last night He was with His disciples, the evening

before His crucifixion, they argued about who among them would be the greatest when Jesus came into His power. One of the twelve He had commissioned was disloyal and betrayed Jesus, revealing his Lord's whereabouts for thirty pieces of silver. And the great majority of followers who heard Jesus' sermons, watched His miracles, saw the love He extended — the great majority shut Him out of their world.

But Jesus didn't say, "Forget it. I'll exclude you from My world too." No! He just kept extending His love — even to those wicked leaders who encouraged others to shout, "Crucify Him!" As these instigators of violence stood around His cross and spat their insults at Him, Jesus prayed, "Father, forgive them, for they do not know what they are doing" (Luke 23:34).

Christ just kept loving people, men and women, people with names, just like the individuals on the list I put together, and like those who would be on your list if you wrote one out. When we in the church are imitating Christ, people don't have to earn our love.

What a difference there would be if the church were comprised of men and women who extended love the way Christ did.

Les Miserables has become the world's most popular musical. Based on Victor Hugo's classic book, it tells the story of a paroled criminal, Jean Valjean, who after being set free, when no one else will befriend him, is finally welcomed into a bishop's home. In spite of this kindness, Valjean steals some silver candlesticks and flees.

Caught by constables, he's taken back to the churchman. "This criminal swears you gave him the silver," they sneer, "but we say he's lying!" The man of God acts surprised. "Why, yes, I did, but I also gave you this tray," he says to his former guest. "Did you forget to take it?"

Because of this loving act done in behalf of a stranger who couldn't be trusted, Valjean is converted and begins a new life. In time, he knows success in business and becomes mayor of a town.

Meanwhile, a police inspector named Javert relentlessly

hunts Valjean because of an earlier parole infraction. In the musical production, when Javert finally finds Valjean he sings, "You have no rights, come with me, No. 24601. Every man is born in sin, every man must choose his way. Men like you can never change!"

But Valjean has changed. Taught by the bishop and the Lord, he is changed in his ways and his name. Now he goes by Father Madeleine. Victor Hugo describes him like this:

> He did a number of good actions, while keeping in the background as they do who commit evil ones. At evening he would steal into dwellings and furtively mount the stairs. A poor wretch would, on returning to his pallet, discover that his door had been forced, or opened, anyway, during his absence. He would cry out, "Some malefactor has been here!" but on entering, the first thing he would spy would be a gold piece on a piece of furniture. The malefactor was Father Madeleine.

If only the same could be written of all who have been converted by the Spirit of Christ to live as our Lord did. If it could be said of me that my love were unconditional. If one could say of you, say of the church, "This is an unusual place, a place where love doesn't have to be earned."

Peter writes in his first epistle, chapter 3, verse 9, "Do not repay evil with evil or insult with insult, but with blessing, because to this you were called."

Have you ever been in a neighborhood when for some reason a bunch of dogs all started barking at the same time? What in the world triggered that? you wonder.

As I've been putting these thoughts together, it's as if all of a sudden I hear church people in doghouses all across the land yapping for their freedom—a great chorus of howling voices saying, "Don't back away, David, this is important. Let people know that it's lonely and scary and cold and miserable out here. Please tell them to let us know the warmth of the family again."

Maybe you're someone who could, at least once, let such a poor soul back into the best family in the world.

Let's go over my point one more time. I'll be very direct.

Far too many people in the church withhold Christlike love from others. Sometimes their reasons are trivial. This practice results in true pain to those who are excluded. I know they haven't been hit or kicked, but the pain is real nevertheless.

This should not be normal behavior for God's family. Our Heavenly Father's love is unconditional. Christ, the Son of God, was the same way.

As spiritual sons and daughters, we are to imitate the love of the Father and the Son. To the degree that we don't, God's family becomes dysfunctional.

We have no excuse. If any family should manifest unconditional love, it should be His. The truth is, we should be a model for all to see—the best family in the world.

Lord,
I praise You for Your unconditional love. You take great pleasure, great joy, great delight in Your children. We don't have to earn Your love. We praise You that we have been made acceptable to You through Christ's ultimate act of love on the cross. Amen.

For Discussion and Reflection

1. How recently have you experienced the pain of being put in someone's "doghouse"?

2. Have you ever been in a congregation where love had to be earned? If so, what was on the price tag?

3. What kind of people do you have the most trouble loving?

4. What do you suppose keeps Christians from extending unconditional love as Jesus did?

5. Based on your experience, would you characterize the church at large as a healthy family or a dysfunctional family? Why?

6. Answer yes or no: Can you name someone you need to let out of the doghouse?

READINGS

"Please say that you love me, please!" Brian's words trailed off into tears as he leaned over the now still form of his father. It was late at night in a large metropolitan hospital. Only the cold, white walls and the humming of a heart monitor kept Brian company. His tears revealed a deep inner pain and sensitivity that had tormented him for years, emotional wounds that now seemed beyond repair.

Brian had flown nearly halfway across the country to be at his father's side in one last attempt to try to reconcile years of misunderstanding and resentment. For years Brian had been searching for his father's acceptance and approval, but they always seemed just out of reach.

Brian's father had been a career Marine officer. His sole desire for Brian when he grew up was that he would follow in his father's footsteps. With that in mind, Brian's father took every opportunity to instill in his son discipline and the backbone he would need when one day he too was an officer.

Words of love or tenderness were forbidden. It was almost as if any slip into a display of warmth might crack the tough exterior Brian's father was trying to create in his son.

Brian was driven by his father to participate in sports and to take elective classes that would best equip him to be an officer. Brian's only praise for scoring a touchdown or doing well in a class was a lecture on how he could and should have done even better.

After graduating from high school, Brian did enlist in the Marine Corps. It was the happiest day of his father's life. However, his joy was short-lived. Cited for attitude problems and a disrespect for orders, his son was soon on report. After weeks of such reports (which included getting into a vicious fight with his drill instructor), Brian was dishonorably discharged from the service as incorrigible.

The news of Brian's dismissal from the Marines dealt a death blow to his relationship with his father. He was no longer welcome in his father's home, and for years there was no contact between them.

During those years, Brian struggled with feelings of inferiority and lacked self-confidence. Even though he was above average in intelligence, he worked at various jobs far below his abilities. Three times he had been engaged—only to break the engagement just weeks before the wedding. Somehow he just didn't believe that another person could really love him. . . .

We began counseling with Brian after he had broken his second engagement. As he peeled away the layers of his past, Brian began to see both his need for his family's blessing and his responsibility for dealing honestly with his parents. That is when the call came from his mother saying that his father was dying from a heart attack.

Brian went immediately to the hospital to see his father. The entire flight he was filled with hope that now, at long last, they could talk and reconcile their relationship. "I'm sure he'll listen to me. I've learned *so* much. I know things are going to change between us." Brian repeated these phrases over and over to himself during the flight. But it was not to be.

Brian's father slipped into a coma a few hours before he arrived. The words that Brian longed to hear for the first time—words of love and acceptance—now could never be spoken. Four hours after Brian arrived at the hospital, his father died without regaining consciousness.

"Dad, please wake up!" Brian's heartbreaking sobs echoed down the hospital corridor. His cries spoke of an incredible sense of loss; not only the physical loss of his father, but, like many others, also the emotional sense of losing any chance of his father's blessing.

The Blessing, Gary Smalley and John Trent, Thomas Nelson, pages 9–11.

■   ■   ■

One of the most common parental family situations which produces perfectionism and depression is unpleaseable parents. Such parents give only conditional love which demands that certain standards are lived up to, top grades achieved, or the highest kind of performance met in athletics or in spiritual life. There is little or no affirmation and plenty of criticism. Even approval is conditional. Encouragement is given but only to stress the fact that "you should have and could have done better." The three A's on the report card aren't mentioned, but the B—"I think you can pull the B up to an A if you try harder." And then when you do try harder and you get that B pulled up to an A and you show the report card to Mother, sure she is going to be pleased, she looks at you for a moment and all of a sudden frowns and says, "My goodness! Where did you get that stain on your jacket! You must have spilled catsup on yourself at the cafeteria. Have you been going around all day looking like that?" Which really translated means, "You lousy ungrateful kid. What kind of a parent are you making me look like before the community?"

Unpleaseable parents and conditional love produce unreachable goals and unattainable standards. Some years ago a lady told me that every time I used the word *obey* or *obedience* in a sermon, she would feel uneasy and guilty. Her mother used to dress her up in the morning for play, in very fancy clothing. And then she would say, "Now, when you go out, don't get any dirt on that pretty dress of yours. I worked hard to iron all those ruffles." You can well imagine what the dress looked like by afternoon and evening. And when the little girl came in, her mother would scold her angrily: "You naughty girl, you never obey me." Absurd, unrealistic, unattainable demands were made. And when they weren't achieved, guilt and punishment were meted out. Since this was a deeply religious home, are you surprised that the child, now a grown woman, struggles with wretched concepts of God, with low self-esteem, and a cloud of guilt?

Healing for Damaged Emotions, David A. Seamands, Victor Books, page 93.

■ ■ ■

It is appropriate here to speak of the harmful effects that a certain kind of religious training can have on children's lives. Although they may speak of love as being of first importance in human affairs, churches often become preoccupied with rigid rules of conduct, betraying a deep mistrust of spontaneity in behavior. The church then tends to condemn any failure to measure up to its standards. Under these circumstances the church creates a community where the members do not experience a free-flowing experience of love for each other but rather one in which they feel on guard and constantly in danger of condemnation.

These attitudes, of course, extend into the family lives of members of the religious group. The result is that some "religious" families are among the most psychologically damaging to their children. Perhaps much of the damaging effect comes because of the confusing message that the judgments and the condemnation are a result of the love of the parents for the child. Such parents often say in effect, "We only say these things to you because we love you so much and want you to be happy." And the fact that the parents *are* sincere and do not recognize that their need to judge, condemn, and mistrust their children is the result of their own self-hate, mistrust of themselves, and resulting fears only makes the message that much more subtle and more difficult for the child to cope with.

Sheri is a young woman who grew up in this kind of a religious family. Her father was an attorney, and he was also a perfectionist and a staunch religionist. Sheri was always made aware that it was very important to him that she succeed in her schooling. In fact she felt his love was dependent on her achievement.

Although she was a very bright girl, Sheri did not respond favorably to these demands. She did not do well in school and dropped out of college, an action of which her father strongly disapproved. Not long thereafter, however, she—on her own initiative—became a skilled legal secretary as a result of her own initiative. She thoroughly enjoyed her work and made a good living for herself.

Instead of being delighted about her success, her father continued to express his disappointment and criticize her for not having made full use of her talents by securing a college degree. Whatever she did, it was never quite good enough.

It is not surprising that Sheri, having been exposed all her life in her "religious" home to such demands, has also tended to see God as demanding an impossible kind of perfection from her. She never thinks of God loving her just as she is. God is made into the image of her father.

Your Fear of Love, Marshall Bryant Hodge, Doubleday, pages 46–48.

■ ■ ■

Things had gone quite well and I was fairly well adjusted to Anderson and to the church. However a tormenting thought kept gnawing away at me, even though I said nothing about it to anyone. Although I would hardly admit harboring it in my heart, it was there like a thorn under my saddle!

During that eventful Sunday morning service I shared this hang-up with the church. "You have never given me the first reason to feel as I have for several months. You have treated me royally and a pastor could not ask for better cooperation and support. However, ever since I have been here I have been plagued by a silly, ridiculous thought. I know you candidated several pastors before I came, and I've been tormented by the thought that had you secured the pastor you really wanted it would have been someone other than I. What I felt you did was to scrape the bottom of the barrel . . . !"

Admittedly that was a crazy thing to say to a congregation and I don't recommend it to my colleagues. Yet as I said it, something very real and wonderful happened to me. It seemed as if the floodgates of heaven were opened between the congregation and me! I simply fell head over heels in love with this church in a depth that I had not known possible before!

I did not realize it, but my wife had some serious problems in loving the church too. Her problem came from a different direction, however. She had loved Lexington so deeply that it pained her grievously when we had to say good-by to such precious friends. "This time," she said, "I'm not going to get hurt when we have to leave." Therefore she determined to play the role of the perfect pastor's wife; except, she was not going to fall so deeply in love with the people. She played her role well.

What both of us had done was to block the flow of love between the church and us. As a result Betty resented Anderson. She didn't like the stores ("I just can't find anything here in this town."). She couldn't stand the bumpy streets. She hated the weather. She with her crazy hang-ups and I with my silly hang-ups made quite a pair. Neither of us knew how the other felt. It is little wonder that so few victories were gained before 1970!

Betty's day of renewal was on its way, too! Two weeks after revival broke, Betty and I found ourselves standing before the church singing a special. We do not profess to be very good singers, but during the revival I believe God could have made a crow sound like a canary!

I sat down after we had sung, but Betty stayed at the pulpit. She always cries when she gives her testimony. That morning she opened her heart as I had opened mine. Suddenly her well-laid plans went up in smoke (holy smoke!), and she experienced the same wonderful, indescribable love that had become mine two weeks earlier.

A New Wind Blowing, Charles R. Tarr, Warner Press, pages 31–33.

■ ■ ■

But how can we define biblical love? It is dangerous to over-simplify, but in a single word it is *Christlikeness*. Biblical love involves demonstrating those attitudes and actions toward others that Christ demonstrated when He came into the world and lived among men. This is why we are told on several occasions in Scripture to "love as Christ loved." (See Eph. 5:2; 5:25; Phil. 2:2.)

Note this—the majority of New Testament directives to "love others" were written to local bodies of believers—not to individual believers *per se*. This is very significant—significant because it is impossible for individual Christians living in isolation to carry out the *functions* of biblical love. It takes a body, a community of believers relating to each other, and encouraging each other, and building each other up to actually "love as Christ loved." (See Eph. 4:16.)

Not only can a "body of Christians" do *functionally* what individual Christians cannot, but also Christians, as a group, have *corporate* strength. And this we need.

We must remember that Jesus Christ was divine! Being God in the flesh, He *was* and *is* love! His capacity for unself-ishness, humility, and self-sacrifice are limitless! Thus, when He went back to heaven, He left not just isolated Christians to carry out His work but believers—people who could express His love through local assemblies and groups. And the most exciting thing is that if these local believers are open to doing the will of God, they can be drawn together in a unique and seldom known or experienced love relationship. Together they can learn to "love as Christ loved."

The Measure of a Church, Gene A. Getz, Regal, pages 33–34.

CHAPTER TWO

BLAMING AND SHAMING

- Have you ever known a family that never had a problem? Where no one ever got seriously sick or was unemployed for an extended period of time? A family of perfect children and perfect in-laws?

Of course not. No family escapes problems.

In fact, a healthy family anticipates problems and develops ways to deal with them. But a dysfunctional family is more likely to fall into a pattern of blaming and shaming when troubles come their way.

Blaming says:

- *"You're* the problem in this family. You drink too much."
- Or "You" (and a shaking finger accompanies that word), *"You* never obey. Everything would be peaceful around here if you just did what you were told."
- Or, arms gesturing in the air, "I can't stand another day with your mother living here! She makes my entire life sour. Nothing's gone right since the day she moved in!"

Blaming someone else. Finding a scapegoat. Pointing a finger in another's direction. Shouting, *"You're* the problem!"

Shaming takes it a step further. Shame attacks, humiliates, sees no good whatever in the person. Shame demeans with accusations like:

- "You're nothing but a lazy bum!"

- "I can't stand anything about you."
- "You're no good. Get out of my sight and don't ever come back here again."
- "I wish you had never been born!"

Now, this is probably obvious, but it's still worth pointing out, that blaming and shaming don't resolve many family problems.

In healthy families, members talk realistically about their tensions and troubles. The emphasis, however, is always on, "What can I do to help improve things?"

Maybe a family member has an annoying pattern of frequently making the others late. In a functional home this person is not called lazy and good for nothing. Instead the others ask, "What can we do to help you get ready on time?" They're openly confronting the situation, but they're not making blaming and shaming statements. And with this healthy approach, the problem person will be much more likely to improve.

BLAMING AND SHAMING IN THE CHURCH

Now let's make a transition to the church, the larger family I'm concerned about. Do congregations ever manifest the dysfunctional trait of blaming and shaming?

You're laughing because you know the answer.

Ever heard a comment like:

- "As far as I'm concerned, the problem in this church is the young people and their music. It's sacrilegious. God won't honor it!"
- "It's the old guard, that's the problem. They're dead set against change of any kind. They'll kill this church if they have their way. That's what they'll do."
- "Maybe he can preach, but he's a lousy pastor! He's never available. To see him you have to get past two secretaries. I remember Pastor Bill. He was warm and friendly. Knew your name. This new guy could care less if someone is hurting."
- "Our crazy denomination is ruining the churches. Sometimes I wonder if there's anyone with a lick of sense in the

entire headquarters. Why, any fourth-grader could do a better job."

That's enough. You get the idea.

The problem is not a new one. Way back in Numbers 14 the people of God got so frustrated with their spiritual leaders they considered stoning them. That's a bit extreme. Who were these incompetents so unqualified for their positions? The answer is *Moses* and *Aaron.*

A similar scenario is recorded in the New Testament. In this situation the roles are reversed. This time it's a group of spiritual leaders who say, "This person we've brought here is evil. We caught her in the very act of adultery." And they force the woman to stand on display in front of a crowd of onlookers. (This takes place in the temple court in Jerusalem where Christ was teaching.) The Pharisees ask our Lord if it's not appropriate to stone the adulteress right then and there.

The scene is one of some confusion. This incident has been a rather rude interruption of Jesus' lecture. He knows the Pharisees have a hidden agenda. They're trying to trap Him. So the tension builds and the anger of those involved is near the surface.

The woman, of course, has been unfairly accused. Everyone knows such a sin requires two people. But she alone is being forced to stand trial for her life. She's naked, whether literally or not hardly matters. That's how she must be feeling—blamed and shamed.

This is a helpful passage in that it's packed with emotion. And that's the nature of blaming and shaming.

When someone in the church family says, "This congregation would be OK if it weren't for all the Hispanics moving into the neighborhood," those words are said with strong feelings.

Or imagine the emotional intensity of words like these: "Everybody knows the board here is notorious for killing our pastors. They always do it. They're power hungry. That's the problem. They're not praying people. They don't seek the mind of the Lord on these matters. They just like to make pastors crawl. I'm right and you know it."

In the church we need to learn to recognize inflammatory statements like these. Very seldom are they true. The people I've known who have served on boards have been sincere Christians for the most part. When neighborhoods change it's not a matter of pure-hearted angels being pushed out to make room for a pack of absolute devils.

Instead, be reminded that many people have developed the nasty habit of always accusing somebody else, of pointing an angry finger at the other guy, of introducing emotionally charged statements into an already difficult situation. And that's because they haven't learned to ask, "What can *I* do to make things better? What responsibility do *I* need to assume?"

Maybe certain board members have been insensitive. But have I prayed for them? Have I graciously confronted the issues through a carefully written letter? Did I even show up to vote at the congregational meeting when the board was elected?

To return to the obvious point made earlier, blaming and shaming don't resolve many problems. This destructive pattern just makes them worse. It's a trait that characterizes *dysfunctional* church families, and unfortunately, it's a common one.

JESUS AND BLAMING AND SHAMING

In the account of the woman taken in adultery, how different Jesus is from the Pharisees. He doesn't overlook the fact that the woman has sinned, but neither does He shame her. My belief is that His carefully chosen words challenge her deeply.

What Christ does is to write on the ground with His finger—maybe the names and sins of her accusers. The account continues:

"If any one of you is without sin, let him be the first to throw a stone at her."

Again He stooped down and wrote on the ground.

At this, those who heard began to go away one at a

time, the older ones first, until only Jesus was left,
with the woman still standing there. Jesus straight-
ened up and asked her, "Woman, where are they?
Has no one condemned you?"
"No one, Sir," she said.
"Then neither do I condemn you," Jesus declared.
"Go now and leave your life of sin."

If you ask me, I'd say that's certainly a better option than
being stoned!
What if you had to choose between being blamed or
shamed? Which option would you select then?
Maybe that's like having to pick between being stoned and
being hanged. Huh?
Blamed or shamed . . . given a chance to think this one
through, most people, I sense, would say, "Being shamed is
worse. I'll take being blamed for something!"
Do you understand the difference by now? Maybe it's good
to review one final time. In a home blame sounds like this.
"The reason our family didn't have a good vacation is because
you didn't make enough money, so we couldn't do anything
special." Blame accuses. It always points the finger at the
other person. It accepts no personal responsibility.
Shame goes one step further. It not only gets a target in
sight, it locks on it. Now there's no escaping. It's only a
matter of time before the victim is destroyed! Not only can
the given person *do* no good, he or she *is* no good. The
individual's very personhood is attacked.

• "You'll never amount to anything!"
• "The brain in your head must be the size of a pea!"
• "Garbage is better than you."

Dr. Sandra Wilson has written a book called *Released from
Shame,* subtitled *Recovery for Adult Children of Dysfunctional
Families.* InterVarsity is the publisher. She writes:

I was standing in line in a crowded public restroom
engaged in one of my favorite hobbies, people-watch-
ing, when I observed a brief interaction between a

mother and daughter. Mother looked harried and weary as she wrestled a huge purse in one hand and a cigarette in the other while waiting for her child to emerge from a toilet stall. When the girl did, the beautiful, bright-eyed daughter marched over to a row of sinks to wash her hands dutifully. On the way, she dropped the jacket she was carrying. Mother snatched it from the floor and shot off a disgusted look which missed its mark since her daughter was engrossed in enthusiastic hand-washing. Water and soapsuds splashed on the mirror, sink, floor, and child while she scrubbed as if about to perform open-heart surgery. Again, Mother released a nonverbal volley of disgust. Finally, the little beauty finished drying her hands and turned around with self-satisfaction and delight bursting from her face, only to be assaulted by her mother's inescapable barrage of displeasure, disgust and disappointment. Mother scolded, punched her child's shoulder and pointed to the water and suds (and then threw in carelessness with her jacket for good measure). She hit her target dead center this time. While the girl was being shoved out the door, her eyes seemed to bleed with sorrow and shame as she cast an apprehensive glance at her angry mother.

The mother's attitudes, actions and words conveyed to her daughter that the child was a disgusting disappointment when she accidentally dropped a jacket and splashed water and soapsuds. In reality, both behaviors are quite unremarkable for a child her age. Mother's behavior betrayed her unrealistic expectations; they needlessly fostered a sense of shame in her child.

By the way, this mother did not show her daughter how to wipe off the mirror and sink after her hand-washing. Instead of teaching the useful skill of cleaning up after oneself, Mother taught another lesson in shame. No doubt, this was a lesson Mother had been taught as a child herself.

Dr. Sandra Wilson continues:

This family vignette illustrates the intergenerational aspect of shame. [Did you get that? It's another characteristic of dysfunctional families. They perpetuate their problems from one generation to the next. Healthy families learn how to make corrections along the line. Back to the book *Released from Shame.*] The mother's furtive glances at those of us in line betrayed her shame at having such an obviously imperfect child. It is likely that, from a young age, Mother's parents taught her the "you should be perfect" lie about herself and her family offspring. And, like a well-trained relay runner, Mother was passing on the family's intergenerational baton of shame. "Shame-passing" seems to be one of the malevolent "skills" taught in dysfunctional families.

Then Dr. Wilson asks:

Do you carry on an intergenerational baton of shame? If your parents shamed you, it is probably because *they* were shamed by *their* parents. And so the wretched relay continues ... "unto the third and fourth generations" and beyond.

Now what happens, again, is that people bring these same dysfunctional family traits, such as blaming and shaming, into the family of God. It's important that we recognize these characteristics for what they are so that we can begin to break the intergenerational cycle. Otherwise the best family in the world, the family of God, becomes dysfunctional. More specifically in this case, blaming and shaming become the norm in the church!

Parishioners point fingers of blame at pastors and say to one another, "Let's face it, the reason the church isn't growing is because he's a lousy preacher." They lock on that issue and to emphasize their point add statements that in reality are shameful. They attack who he is, so that before too long the pastor can do no good—at least in their eyes.

Or ministers blame the problems of the church on the lack of commitment of those in the pew. "My people don't pray like they should." And before long he's saying they don't give like they should, or know the Scriptures like they should, or carry on the work of the church like they should. After a while the pastor can't think of anything his parishioners do right! He says to fellow pastors, "This is the worst excuse for a congregation I've ever seen," which is a shame-inducing remark.

And with neither side assuming any responsibility for what it might do to make things better, how can the congregation ever become whole? What I'm saying is that sometimes *church* families pass on the intergenerational baton of shame (to quote Sandra Wilson) and the wretched relay continues.

As healthy families are on their guard against the blame-shame syndrome (they nip it in the bud), so healthy congregations are as well.

This doesn't mean constructive criticism has no place in the church, or that people are allowed to say only "nice" things. It doesn't mean ministers can't preach about sin, or that nobody in the church will ever get angry or have their feelings hurt. This doesn't mean there won't be any misunderstandings in a congregation.

But thinking one person is the cause of everything that's wrong—this is not good. Making insensitive remarks or talking behind someone's back—that's not good either. You shouldn't be allowed to point an accusing finger at others and never ask yourself, "What *can I do to make things* better?" Let me quote our Lord. He had such a marvelous way of picturing things. There's obviously humor here. His illustration goes beyond being ludicrous:

> Why do you look at the speck of sawdust in your brother's eye and pay no attention to the plank in your own eye? How can you say to your brother, "Let me take the speck out of your eye," when all the time

there is a plank in your own eye? You hypocrite, first take the plank out of your own eye, and then you will see clearly to remove the speck from your brother's eye (Matt. 7:3-5).

A HELPFUL PRAYER

I'd like to share a short prayer with you. Try praying it every day for a month. It's preventive maintenance, to remind you to avoid the blame-shame trap:

Father,
I know that no church is perfect,
So help me not to be surprised when problems arise.
Keep me from pointing a finger of blame at others;
Guard my tongue from shameful remarks.
Grant me the courage to do my part to make our church a better place.
And thank You for graciously allowing me to be part of the best family in the world.
Amen.

What do you think? Would praying that simple prayer be a good reminder for you to avoid blaming and shaming others, and to help you assume personal responsibility for what you can do to make things better? Then put the prayer to use.

You know, when problems come up, there's something in us that almost automatically wants to get the focus off ourselves and what we've done (or not done), and to spotlight the other person instead. That is true of me, and I've seen this pattern in the lives of many of my peers, good men and women in ministry.

Maybe that tendency is true of you as well.

But again, the blame-shame syndrome is destructive. It almost always makes matters worse. It's a characteristic of dysfunctional families.

Conversely, when problems arise in healthy families, each member assumes responsibility for what he or she can do to make things better. May that be so in the best of all families, the church of Jesus Christ.

Lord,
I praise You for the tenderness of Your mercy. Your nature is not to point a harsh finger of blame, or to shame us when we sin. But You surprise us with Your kindness—and gently call us to Your better way. Amen.

For Discussion and Reflection

1. Explain the difference between blaming and shaming.

2. Is blaming-shaming really a problem in churches, or is this book making too much of it? Explain your answer.

3. What happens when, instead of blaming, someone says, "I'm going to assume responsibility for what I can do to make things better"?

4. What do you think is the difference between constructive criticism of the church and the dysfunctional pattern of blaming and shaming?

5. What verses or passages of Scripture come to mind that relate to this dysfunction?

6. How might praying the prayer suggested in this chapter help you become sensitive to the problem of blaming and shaming?

7. Will you make use of the prayer every day for the next month? Why or why not?

READINGS

The blamer with the accusingly pointed finger has found the most convenient way to excuse himself of all responsibility, or escape detection of her part in the problem: Finger the foe. Fix the blame. Assign the guilt. Define whose problem it is. Lay the full responsibility at the other's doorstep. If the partner willingly grovels, the interaction is complete. Every blamer seeks a placater; every guilty victim, a tyrant. It takes two to continue these cyclical psychodramas. It takes one to quit.

The need to blame rises from the fear of being blamed. Those who frequently blame others are avoiding the pain of the chronic inner conflict between a blaming tyrant and a bleeding victim. Rather than suffer the attacks of the ruthless censor preying on the self, one turns the blame outward.

Before raising the condemning finger, the blamer feels blame within. To follow this urge to punish the self is intolerable so the punishment is turned outward. This rage against all inconvenience, all failure, all imperfection, all that goes wrong in life flares instantly and urgently within, flashes in the eyes and burns in the words. Why feel blamed when you can blame?

Blame is evasive. Rather than facing the difficulty and work at resolving it, it seeks transfer of the total to the other, to stir up shame, pain, self-rejection in the other hoping to stimulate self-correction by the other. Such negative means produce negative feelings and lead to negative results. Growth comes from owning responsibility, not from accepting blame.

Blame is censure. Rather than pointing toward the future and inviting change and growth, blame penalizes the past and punishes the person for the acts, whether real or fantasized. Change and healing come from responsibility thinking, not from figuring out whose fault.

Blame is powerless. Because it is punitive, negative, evasive, blaming tends to merely increase the inner frustrations and conflicts in both parties which contributed to the original breakdown in communication or relationship. This leads to cyclical criticisms of each other whether expressed in words or acted out in silence or submission.

When Caring Is Not Enough, David Augsburger, Regal, pages 95–96.

■ ■ ■

Dysfunctional parents contribute to the problem by heaping blame upon their children. "You're the cause of all the problems around here," is a rough statement for an eleven-year-old girl to deal with. Directly or indirectly, they feel responsible. "My dad left my mom because of me," or "If I behaved differently, Mom wouldn't drink." The sexually abused may think, "I feel guilty because there are times I responded sexually to my dad's assaults." "I can't get over the guilt I feel for sometimes feeling close to my mother when she fondled me." We adults know children shouldn't feel guilty when things happen they can't control. But it's not so obvious to children.

Unfinished Business: Helping Adult Children Resolve Their Past, Charles Sell, Multnomah, page 90.

■ ■ ■

When a child is born to these shame-based parents, the deck is stacked from the beginning. The job of parents is to model.

Modeling includes how to be a man or woman; how to relate intimately to another person; how to acknowledge and express emotions; how to fight fairly; how to have physical, emotional and intellectual boundaries; how to communicate; how to cope and survive life's unending problems; how to be self-disciplined; how to love oneself and another. Shame-based parents cannot do any of these. They simply don't know how.

Healing the Shame That Binds You, John Bradshaw, Health Communications, Inc., pages 25–26.

■ ■ ■

A curse is not merely a harmful wish or prediction but it has destructive effects upon those who believe it. A curse has inherent power that causes misfortune to occur in ways we may not understand.

In Proverbs 18:21 we are warned that life and death are in the power of the tongue. The tongue is further described in James 3:8-9 as being a "restless evil, full of death-bringing poison" with which "we bless the Lord and Father, and . . . curse men who were made in God's likeness!" In our work with abusive families, we have found several common statements that directly perpetuate the cycle of abuse. These statements are handed down from generation to generation; and when believed, their power produces the effect of a curse.

"When you grow up, you'll have children of your own, and then you'll get what you deserve. They'll pay you back for what you did to me."

When a child in an abusive family grows up hearing this statement, marries and has children, he will sense within himself that the time has come for the fulfillment of this curse. As this person consciously or unconsciously recalls the predicted curse, the child will be seen as the assigned enemy who has come to make him pay. When the child begins to demand attention by crying, whining, or demanding constant care, the parent will become tired and frustrated, interpreting the child's behavior as deliberate persecution.

One mother said, "Tommy knows when I lie down to take a nap. He always begins to scream, and he won't stop until I pick him up! I know he's only two years old, but I don't think he wants me to have a minute's peace. It makes me so angry! I feel like he has it in for me. Oh, well, Mother always said I'd get what I deserve, and he's sure giving it to me."

If a parent feels that he deserves to be abused by his own child, he will allow the child's abusive behavior to escalate, and he will not consistently discipline his child. Because he believes that his child is an instrument of revenge, he will allow misbehavior to continue until he can no longer bear it. Anger will finally consume him and then abuse will occur.

One man, describing his mounting frustration, said, "My three-year-old son whined and cried for so long that I finally couldn't stand it anymore. I warned him a few times, but he just kept screaming. Before I knew it, I had jerked him up and had begun to hit him. The longer I hit, the harder I hit. I hit him all over his body, and I didn't even realize what I had done until I had stopped. The next day, he was covered with bruises. I'm afraid to ever touch him again. I'm afraid I might kill him next time."

The truth is that no child, even though he may demand attention or misbehave, knows what your parents thought you deserved. A child cannot meet an assignment to "pay you back." The problem comes when you interpret the normal behavior of children as a personal attack upon you. In order to break the power of this curse, it is important to get information about what a child is able to do at a given age and to see your child within the framework. It helps to understand typical behavior that occurs at given ages and stages of childhood. As you gain knowledge, you will be able to see that your child is simply a child, not an instrument of revenge.

The truth is that your children were sent to you as a love gift from God. Psalm 127:3-5 says, "Sons are a heritage from the Lord, children a reward from Him. Like arrows in the hands of a warrior are sons born in one's youth. Blessed is the man whose quiver is full of them." Ask God to help you see your children as His blessing to you. Thank Him for them daily. As you do this, you will begin to see them as a gift and not as a curse.

My Father's Child, Lynda D. Elliott and Vicki L. Tanner, Wolgemuth and Hyatt, pages 127–129.

■ ■ ■

Now we all know what Jesus meant by the mote in the other person's eye. It is some fault which we fancy we can discern in him; it may be an act he has done against us, or some attitude he adopts towards us. But what did the Lord Jesus mean by the beam in our eye? I suggest that the beam in our eye is simply our unloving reaction to the other man's mote. Without doubt there is a wrong in the other person. But our reaction to that wrong is wrong too! The mote in him has provoked in us resentment, or coldness, or criticism, or bitterness, or evil speaking, or ill will—all of them variants of the basic ill, unlove. And that, says the Lord Jesus, is far, far worse than the tiny wrong (sometimes quite unconscious) that provoked it. A mote means in the Greek a little splinter, whereas a beam means a rafter. And the Lord Jesus means by this comparison to tell us that our unloving reaction to the other's wrong is what a great rafter is a to a little splinter! Every time we point one of our fingers at one another and say, "It's your fault," three of our fingers are pointing back at us. God have mercy on us for the many times when it has been so with us and when in our hypocrisy we have tried to deal with the person's fault, when God saw there was this thing far worse in our own hearts.

But let us not think that a beam is of necessity some *violent* reaction on our part. The first beginning of a resentment is a beam, as is also the first flicker of an unkind thought, or the first suggestion of unloving criticism. Where that is so, it only distorts our vision and we shall never see our brother as he really is, beloved of God.

The Calvary Road, Roy and Revel Hession, Christian Literature Crusade, pages 83–85.

CHAPTER THREE

UNHEALTHY COMPARISONS AND COMPETITION

• Your sister is truly beautiful, and you're glad for her. But it hurts when you hear people refer to you as the plain daughter in the family.

Or your brother has been highly successful. Businesswise, he has the Midas touch. Everything he touches turns to gold. His money opens up a lot of worlds for him, worlds that you know little about as a junior high school teacher. Most people acquainted with your parents think of your brother as the more successful son. You resent that!

Comparisons. In a family the pain of comparisons can sometimes last an entire lifetime.

Do comments like these sound familiar? Does the sting of words like these hurt you?

"Your sister made honor roll *every* time."

"He worked harder than you did. That's why your brother made the first team."

"When your cousin was your age, my dear, she not only was married, she had two children!"

"What do I think about your traveling halfway around the world to some unheard-of country to get them to change religions? I think I'm glad none of my other children are going to ask their family and friends to give money to help them do that!"

COMPARISONS AND UNHEALTHY FAMILIES

Unhealthy comparisons like these are another characteristic of dysfunctional families. Someone else is always more athletic, or smarter, or better looking, or more talented, or less of an embarrassment.

It hurts to be told in one way or another that you don't measure up. It hurts deeply.

How would you like to be part of a larger family where the competition is even more intense? A family that has many additional members, offering a greater number of opportunities for comparisons?

"Forget it," you respond. "That's the last thing I want!" The exceptionally gifted might see that as a challenge. But for most of us, the very idea is painful. We don't need to be reminded that in many ways we don't measure up.

A HEALTHY FAMILY MODEL

But what if this is a healthy family? What if it's one where the uniqueness of who you are as a person is understood and affirmed? Suppose that you're an artist, you're not judged on the basis of your athletic prowess. If you're a good teacher, you're not made to feel inferior because you don't earn a lot of money. If you're skilled at working with little children, that's OK; you don't have to be a great writer as well. If you *can* do both, terrific. But this distinctive family I'm describing knows that no one can be good at everything.

So the emphasis in this special family is on finding the uniqueness of each member. There isn't a comparison game going on. Sound good? In this family, when a person discovers his or her true self, everyone rejoices. They say, "How wonderful! That's the perfect role for you at this point in your life."

Here's the ideal as described by the Apostle Paul. In 1 Corinthians 12, Paul is writing about the family of God, the body of Christ, the church. Read his words as if you'd never read them before:

Now the body is not made up of one part but of many.

If the foot should say, "Because I am not a hand, I do not belong to the body," it would not for that reason cease to be part of the body. And if the ear should say, "Because I am not an eye, I do not belong to the body," it would not for that reason cease to be part of the body. If the whole body were an eye, where would the sense of hearing be? If the whole body were an ear, where would the sense of smell be? But in fact God has arranged the parts of the body, every one of them, just as He wanted them to be. If they were all one part, where would the body be? As it is, there are many parts, but one body.

The eye cannot say to the hand, "I don't need you!" And the head cannot say to the feet, "I don't need you!" [Your head wouldn't say that to your feet, would it? "Don't need you, feet—get lost."] On the contrary, those parts of the body that seem to be weaker are indispensable, and the parts that we think are less honorable we treat with special honor. And the parts that are unpresentable are treated with special modesty, while our presentable parts need no special treatment. But God has combined the members of the body and has given greater honor to the parts that lacked it [restated, if God had His way, He'd see to it that the greater attention or honor went to the parts that were lacking or seemed less worthy by comparison], so that there should be no division in the body, but that its parts should have equal concern for each other. If one part suffers, every part suffers with it; if one part is honored, every part rejoices with it (1 Cor. 12:14-26).

That's the way it should be in the family of God. Look at it this way. Say a husband and wife have one especially gifted child. I'm thinking of one such couple whose high-school-age daughter is incredibly skilled. She has won countless awards. She's just a phenomenal achiever. But it's important for these parents to give equal—if not greater—attention to their other two children whose abilities are more ordinary. Otherwise, the load of comparison might end up being too heavy for the less-exceptional brother and sister to bear.

So in the family of God, a great family with more than its share of truly gifted members, it's critical, as Paul points out, to treat those whose abilities are less spectacular, with added honor, perhaps even more attention. Otherwise, it's conceivable that they could experience more pain from being in the family of God than what they might in their natural family.

The church must not be a place that spotlights the gifted and ignores the unexceptional. It should be a family where each person is seen as special and important, an individual with a God-designed role to be discovered and nurtured and applauded. And may the Lord forgive us if we make anyone feel unneeded, or left out, or of little comparative value, or only a half brother or half sister.

But let's face it, this happens.

UNFAIR COMPARISONS

• Sometimes Christians are made to feel that the people who give big donations are more important than those who give small ones. Jesus made it obvious this wasn't true. Remember the widow's mite? But the illusion remains.

• Sometimes we act as if the people who preach should be treated better than the people who do janitorial work.

• Or we subconsciously believe that those who go on visitation are more committed to Christ than those who sing in the choir.

• The Lord's hand is more evident on the big-name recording artists than it is on those who sing with a stock accompaniment tape.

• Those who win church elections have to be more saintly than those who lose.

• Those who teach the senior high Sunday School class are more loyal to the church than those involved in a parachurch Campus Life club ministry.

• Those who attend church every time there's a meeting

are more committed than those who usually only come on Sunday morning.

• Paid church staff are more spiritual than volunteer workers.

• Or those who have known and developed their gifts ever since they were young people in the church deserve more respect than new Christians who haven't the faintest idea what gifts of the Holy Spirit are, much less which ones are theirs.

The human way is to reward those who already have a decided advantage—those who were born beautiful, or intelligent, or unusually talented, or wealthy, or who inherited a last name everyone respects. (I grant you that becoming mature is hard enough for them. Probably a lot of privileged families are dysfunctional, and foster competition and unhealthy comparisons.)

But pity all the others, the many folk with so little going for them, usually having been brought up in dysfunctional families too. It's sad if they can't find a place of honor. They shouldn't have to search to no avail for a family where the parts that seem weaker are recognized as being indispensable, and the parts we think are less honorable are treated with special honor, and the parts that are unpresentable are treated with special care.

A PLACE FOR SPECIAL CARE
Praise the Lord that He's provided such a place. That place is the marvelous family of God, the best family in the world—if we act the way we're supposed to.

The other Sunday in church I had a freak accident. We meet in a high school auditorium because the congregation has outgrown our original sanctuary, but we're not quite large enough yet to start another building program.

I was sitting there paying attention to the pastor's message. I had leaned my arm on the left armrest. You know what seats look like in a high school auditorium. Well, suddenly there was a noise like a loud snap, and at that moment, the left side of my seat gave out from under me. My arm slipped sideways and my chest slammed down on that wooden armrest.

The impact made a sound loud enough for a number of people to hear it and turn around. I managed not to cry out, even though it really hurt!

I later found out I had cracked a rib! Now when I turn in certain ways my injury immediately lets me know that all is not right!

Have you ever injured a part of your body, broken a little toe maybe? Chipped a tooth and exposed a nerve? If so, you'll be able to identify with my experience.

You see, I've learned how to favor that sore spot. I do what the Apostle Paul writes about and give special honor to the wishes of that weaker part—to say, "That's all right, Mr. Rib. If the normal morning routine of thirty-five sit-ups bothers you that much, I'll just forgo the exercises until you're feeling better about them!"

That's because each part of my body needs to do its job well, including my abdominal muscles. But each part also needs to be concerned about the other members of the body, including my ribs.

Here's another recent experience that, in an even more intimate way, illustrates the truth I'm sharing. My mother is almost eighty. She's still a very beautiful woman. Mom is under nursing care because she has Alzheimer's disease. One of the symptoms is that her memory is faulty. She can't tell time anymore, or dial a phone, or remember which room is hers when she goes down the hall. She can't work with numbers in any way.

Mom still plays the piano well. And she recognizes all the family members. Her face lights up whenever I visit. "This is my son, David," she used to say. Now it might be, "This is my brother, David," or "my dear father, David."

She was an editor all her professional life, and she still corrects my grammar. But frequently now she mixes up words, and that distresses her. She says, "I'm all right, but I have a sore elbow," when she means knee.

"It doesn't matter, Mom," I tell her. "You're doing beautifully. We can cover for you. You don't remember when Dad's coming by tonight? Here, I'll write it down for you. Dad's coming by tonight at 7:30. It's right here on the pad." Then later, "Don't worry about where you put the pad, Mom. Here, let me get it for you.

"Your daughter, Donna, is coming up from Nashville in six more days. One, two, three, four, five, six. Sounds wonderful, right? And that's fine—I know I already told you, but I don't mind telling you a hundred times if need be. It's just great to have you here when I come by. I'm glad I can bring you joy because that's what you give to me. No, I'm not too busy. Stopping by here is the highlight of my day."

You see, that's what a family is for. We're there to do for each other what needs to be done. The healthy elbow can't say to the injured knee, "I don't need you anymore, pal!" (That's 1 Cor. 12—with a few alterations.) Again, those parts of the family that seem to be weaker are actually indispensable. We don't want to part with them. The members some might think less honorable we treat with greater honor. And the member suffering with a disease like Alzheimer's we treat very lovingly and with special care. Otherwise, what does it mean to be a family or a body?

Of course, what Paul is writing about in this passage is the church. And again, he wants each member to know what part he or she plays and to do that well. That in itself is a big job to pull off, to get everybody to the place where they know they fit.

Thank the Lord for all the work that's been done in the church in the last several decades to help people discover how they're uniquely gifted to serve Christ. But Christians also need to be concerned about the value of other members of the body, especially those who take a little longer to discover their unique contribution.

We can't be satisfied to say (or think), "All that matters is me, and I'm doing quite well, thank you. I'm teaching Sunday School now," or, "Did you notice I just got elected to the board?" or, "I sing in the choir—you should have picked that up by this time," or, "I planted the flowers that line the front walk to the sanctuary. I know you don't appreciate all the work that took. I mean, it's one of the few jobs in this church where someone literally gets his hands dirty!"

If "I" remains the center of focus, that's bad! We must be concerned about all parts of the body. Otherwise, the church is like a Mr. America contestant competing in long pants because his chest and arms are strong and look good, but his legs are scrawny and chicken-like.

What about you? How much do you think about the good of the whole body in contrast to what you personally are getting out of the church? I believe many of us in the body of Christ need to recapture this attitude: "It's my privilege to care about you; I mean, you're family too! You're important to us all. The Lord has you here for a reason. You have a part to play that should make us all better people!"

The point I'm making is that as a member of the body of Christ you need to do your part well, but you also need to be concerned about the other members of the body.

Again, research shows that dysfunctional families are characterized by unhealthy comparisons and even outright competition. "I'm smarter (or prettier or more athletic or better at making money) than you are. Just compare houses (or cars or jobs or wardrobes) and you'll see!" But what kind of a family is that? The experts would say it's a sick family.

CHRISTLIKE BEHAVIOR
What I'm pointing out is that just because someone knows she is a good musician doesn't mean she is Christlike in the way she relates to others. It simply means she's a good singer, maybe a dynamic singer. Hopefully, she's also a good family member.

Because an exceptional athlete is a Christian doesn't mean he necessarily is Christlike in his relationships to others. He may be a star as an individual but a lousy team member.

Because someone is good at talking on his feet doesn't mean he's Christlike in the way he treats people. He's just good with words. Christ was good with words, but He was much more than that. It's the "much more" we're attempting to grow into.

Here's Paul in Ephesians 4:15-16. "Instead, speaking the truth in love, we will in all things grow up into Him who is the Head, that is, Christ. From Him the whole body, joined and held together by every supporting ligament, grows and builds itself up in love, as each part does its work."

So yes, what we do as individual parts in the church is important, but love for one another is equally important. Aim for both.

Here's the same truth underscored in Romans 12:3-6, 10. "For by the grace given me I say to every one of you: Do not think of yourself more highly than you ought, but rather think of yourself with sober judgment, in accordance with the measure of faith God has given you. Just as each of us has one body with many members, and these members do not all have the same function, so in Christ we who are many form one body, and each member belongs to all the others. We have different gifts, according to the grace given us. . . . Be devoted to one another in brotherly love. Honor one another above yourselves."

Perhaps you're thinking, "David, you know what our body is like? It's not a cracked rib, a chipped tooth, or a busted toe. It's more like a car crash victim with all kinds of broken bones and bleeding wounds. To be healed, this body needs an emergency medical team, not someone who knows little more about healing than kissing a child's finger to make it better!"

I know what you mean. Christ faced the same problem. He encountered broken people, broken families, all the time He walked the earth. He didn't heal everybody who was broken or diseased or demoralized. He just did what He could.

So I'm challenging you to show compassion as Christ did—especially to those hurting parts of Christ's body nearest you. Be sensitive to them and do what you can, for Jesus' sake. Obey His Word and in doing so make certain that people still feel His family is the best family around.

In Shakespeare's *Much Ado about Nothing,* Dogberry, a rather simple-minded constable, intends to say, "Comparisons are odious," which means they're disgusting or offensive. But instead he says, "Comparisons are odorous," meaning they have a sweet-smelling fragrance. So Dogberry gets it backward, and in doing so, he gets a laugh from the audience for saying something so silly (Act 3, Scene 5, line 18).

Maybe in the church we sometimes get it backward, thinking comparisons are like perfume as long as we come out smelling good. The truth is, unhealthy comparisons are odious.

When the nose says, "Mr. Ear, I don't need you," that's disgusting and offensive and a mark of a dysfunctional family.

Rather, the nose should say, "To smell, the body needs me. To hear, the body needs you, Mr. Ear. I need you and you need me! And both of us need the many other parts if this body is to function as the Lord intended it would."

Lord,
I praise You for Your marvelous originality in creating Your children. You delight in our uniqueness. We don't have to compete with one another, because You have given each of us a special blend of abilities to accomplish Your work through us. Amen.

For Discussion and Reflection

1. What kinds of unhealthy comparisons have you observed in your family or other families?

2. Describe what the opposite of this dysfunctional trait looks like. If comparisons and competition in a family are usually unhealthy, what signs might show that a family functions well in this area?

3. Have you been aware on occasion of unhealthy comparisons in the family of God? What is one example?

4. Suppose someone contended that the church spotlights those with obvious gifts, but ignores Paul's instructions to show greater honor to the members who lack attention. Would you agree or disagree?

5. How concerned is the average church person that all members of God's family discover what their gifts are and where they can best be used? How concerned are you?

6. What are some ways the family of God might encourage one another to discover and use their gifts?

READINGS

Individuality is prized in the healthy family. There are no "different" children in the sense of "Tim is our different one," or "We don't know where we got Karen." Remarks such as these, even though they're usually made by parents in a jesting tone, are often veiled put-downs of differences. The healthy family makes room for a wide variety of personalities, interests, and differences. This family may include a scholar, an athlete, and an artist, and instead of emphasizing differences, it emphasizes the richness that this diversity brings to the family. "We're so lucky," said a mother in front of her family at a reunion, "because we get to be part of a lot of different things like soccer, drama, and jazz band. If all of us were alike, think what we'd be missing."

Yet, we often foster conformity as a value in our culture. In writing on this, Reverend Thomas E. Legere says, "A sure way to strike terror in the heart of a parent is to tell him or her that their child is not 'well adjusted.' In this country in particular, we seem to regard 'adjustment' as one of our national values. . . . It seems to me that making a fetish out of 'adjustment' is a sure way to encourage mediocrity. Greatness in any way, shape or form is usually accomplished by people who are a little bit different than the rest of the world." He said that Albert Einstein was always considered weird, "When he went up to receive his Nobel Prize he wore a nice tuxedo. But he forgot to wear socks or tie his shoes. Was he 'well adjusted?' "

Traits of a Healthy Family, Delores Curran, Ballantine Books, pages 91–92.

■ ■ ■

One of the great encouragements of the Bible is seen in the diverse natures of the men Jesus called to be His disciples— James and John, the sons of thunder; Peter, the impulsive one; Andrew, the friendly one; Philip, the practical man; Nathanael, the visionary; Matthew, the accountant. And yes, even Judas, the businessman who betrayed Jesus. Each was unique. Jesus never made comparisons. He dealt with His disciples as individuals and loved them as they were. He respected their differences.

When God created us in His own image, He purposely designed us with distinct personalities. No poor imitations or cookie-cutter creations for Him. No reprints, replicas, or reproductions. Each person would be an original, one of a kind, with the inherent worth of an original work of art crafted by the Master Craftsman. Is it any wonder then that He expects us to honor one another as the genuine article—*His* workmanship?

Long before psychology existed or before the world existed, for that matter, individuality thrived in the Trinity. The Father, Son, and Holy Spirit are three distinct personalities with separate functions and unique characteristics, and yet they are one. By their very differences they complement one another in the Godhead.

The Child in Each of Us, Richard W. Dickinson and Carole Gift Page, Victor Books, page 19.

■ ■ ■

To be sure, we all have different abilities, looks, personalities, and qualities. We were all made to be something special and unique. The more that truth sinks in and becomes a part of our minds, the less we will compare. And the less we compare, the more we can gaze upon others with love.

Suggested Application. If you're caught in the snare of making comparisons, it might result from your being blind to and ungrateful for what God has already provided. Out of a thankless heart you compare.

To make the necessary reversal of attitude, one possibility would be to keep a notebook called "God's Gifts" or "Gifts God Has Given Me." In it keep a running list of all that Christ has graciously provided.

On top of your list, write down the fact that God made you into a special, unique person. Then add all of those qualities and strengths He has been working overtime to build into your life. Include acts of love, family members, friends, opportunities, and other blessings.

Having launched this project, review your list once or twice each day. As you do, gratitude will well up inside you toward Christ for all of His gifts. Then you will lose your need and drive to compare.

How to Have a Better Relationship with Anybody, James Hilt, Moody Press, pages 77–78.

■ ■ ■

The church is primarily and fundamentally a body designed to express through each individual member the life of an indwelling Lord and is equipped by the Holy Spirit with gifts designed to express that life. It follows that there could hardly be anything more abortive or pathetic than a church which fails to understand this and substitutes instead the business methods, organizational proceedings and pressure politics of the world to accomplish its work. That is a certain recipe for frustration and ultimate death. But to rediscover the divine program for the operation of a church is exciting and challenging.

To become aware that God himself has equipped you—yes, you—with a uniquely designed pattern of spiritual gifts and has placed you exactly where he wants you in order to minister those gifts, is to enter a whole new dimension of exciting possibility. In all the world there is no experience more satisfying and fulfilling than to realize that you have been the instrument of the divine working in the lives of others. Such an experience awaits any true Christian who is willing to give time and thought to the discovery and understanding of his pattern of gifts, and will submit himself to the authority of the Head of the body, who reserves to himself the right to coordinate and direct its activities.

Body Life, Ray C. Stedman, Regal, pages 51–52.

■ ■ ■

Should he tell the Juggling Master? But how could he bear to have his place taken from him and given to another? What would happen if he followed his inner count? What disaster would befall him?

With sagging shoulders, the Apprentice Juggler walked home from the practice field. Later, with lagging feet, he made his way to the huge clearing in Deepest Forest. Here the Great Celebration always took place, surrounded by the circle of Sacred Flames.

The subjects of the King were beginning to gather in Inmost Circle. The Sacred Flames had been lit, and they flickered and danced in a huge ring. Rangers in their dark blue cloaks stood posted around the flames. The music of celebration had begun.

The Apprentice Juggler watched as celebrants walked through the gateway of flames into Inmost Circle: "making entrance," the ceremony was called. He saw each one become real as he or she did so, for the Sacred Flames showed persons not as they seemed, but as they truly were. All disguises were gone.

The laughter and the music and the joy within the flames called to the Apprentice Juggler. But he held himself back. How could he make entrance with this hidden thing in his heart? Wouldn't his secret be revealed when he became real?

The funny old Caretaker walked through the flames. His

form dimmed for a moment in the bright light. Then he made entrance. He became tall, straight, broad-shouldered, wearing the dark blue cloak and silver clasp of a Ranger. Caretaker was not what he seemed. He had become Ranger Commander, chief protector of the park and intimate adviser to the King himself.

The Apprentice Juggler squirmed. He remembered how Caretaker had found him, as a young child, hungry and abandoned, and had taken him to Mercie, who had loved and nursed him. He remembered how Caretaker and Mercie hated dark and hidden things.

He decided to wait for the Juggling Master and tell him the hidden secret that his inner count was different and dangerous to the troupe. The Apprentice Juggler would ask him to choose another for the finale. It was the only way.

A sob shook his shoulders. Nevermore the feel of the batons or the thrill of tumbling objects. Nevermore the weight of the ball popping into his palm, then popping out. Nevermore the wonderful rhythm of the troupe.

They would give his place to another. What would become of him? Where would he belong? The young man knew he would never make a good baker or gardener or forester. He couldn't stand singing or dancing. He had absolutely no desire to be a Ranger. The only thing he had ever wanted to do was make balls and clubs and rings and batons and eggs — unboiled — dance.

In anger, the Apprentice Juggler tossed the balls he held. This time he kept his own count. Sure enough, the balls moved at awkward intervals. The juggling was not smooth. The rising and falling rhythms were hazardous. He had to tell his secret. He would never be like the other jugglers.

A beggar was approaching the circle of fire. The man wore a brown cloak with a hood that covered his face. He carried a staff and limped. "Alms! Alms!" he cried. "Pennies for the poor! The poor!"

The beggar stopped by the boy and asked, "Juggler, are you performing in the Great Celebration?"

The young man shook his head. Suddenly he wanted to

stutter out his secret. He wanted to say, "I have something hidden in my heart."

The beggar motioned for him to step closer and whispered, "I saw you juggling just now. Keep your own count. Listen to the rhythm of your own timing."

The Apprentice Juggler was amazed. How could a beggar know his count was wrong when he had guarded the truth from everyone?

The beggar laughed. He said, "I understand. My rhythm is different, too." With that, the beggar turned to make entrance.

The boy heard the Rangers shout, "To the King! To the Restoration!" The form of the man was dimmed in the flames, then he stepped into Inmost Circle. A cry of recognition went up. People came running to welcome the new arrival. They shouted greeting and called to one another.

The Apprentice Juggler gasped. He had not been prepared for this becoming. The man stood there, changed. He was as tall as Ranger Commander and handsome. The light from the flames reflected as gold glints in his hair. He bent and swung a little child up to his broad shoulders. Mercie, young and beautiful, now that she had made entrance, ran from a place within the circle and took his hand. She called to her husband, Ranger Commander, who came and saluted the King.

The beggar is the King, thought the Apprentice Juggler. *He had said, "Keep your own count."*

The King raised his one hand, still holding the little child on his shoulder with the other. His voice commanded, "Let the celebration begin!"

In response to the King's command, the musicians began to play a joyful foot-tapping melody. It called the subjects out of Deepest Forest, through the Sacred Flames, and into Inmost Circle. The jugglers were gathering at the heart of the celebration. The King and his followers circled 'round them. Everyone clapped in time with the music.

The whole troupe was juggling, each on their own. Some tossed balls. Some looped rings. Then it was time for the Apprentice Juggler's first solo act. All the others stopped.

The young man's heart was in his throat. What if a ball dropped? What if he tripped? What if he couldn't control his count? Then he remembered the Beggar King and his words, "Listen to the rhythm of your own timing."

He listened. A new count was rising in him, his own count. Joy came tumbling. It filled his hands, his heart. The count was different from anything he had ever heard. *Throw☆ Throw-catch☆Catch☆Catchcatch☆Throw; Throw☆ Throwcatch ☆Catch☆Catchcatch☆Throw.*

He tossed an orange high, high into the air. Then another and another. He caught the first orange right before it hit the ground. The crowd gasped. He caught and tossed the next falling one off his foot. The people gasped again; then they laughed. The Apprentice Juggler dived for the third, tossed it, turned a somersault, caught the next inches off the ground, popped it back up into the air. The crowd roared.

He heard murmurs. "Oh! He's wonderful!" "I've never seen a juggler like him before!" "How different!"

He went on listening to the inner timing. *Throw☆ Throw-catch☆Catch☆Catchcatch☆Throw.* He juggled and somersaulted and dived and counted. Finally, he was done. The crowd laughed. They clapped. They yelled hurrah and stamped their feet and hands.

The Apprentice Juggler bowed. He stood straight and bowed again. This time when he looked up, he was looking directly into the eyes of the King.

The King was smiling his approval.

"A clown! A clown!" someone was crying. It was the Juggling Master.

"You have the rhythm of a clown!" he crowed. "You look like you can't do it. . . . You look like you might drop something. But you don't! A clown is the best juggler of all!"

The Juggling Master became stern. He shook the juggler's shoulders. "Why didn't you tell me your rhythm was different?"

"Be-be-because," stammered the young man between shakes. "I-I thought I would lose my place in the troupe."

The Juggling Master stopped shaking him. "Lose your

place? Find your proper place, rather. Didn't you know that in the Great Celebration, all who desire a place, find a place?"

With that, the Juggling Master put his head back and laughed. "A juggler with the instinct of a clown! Oh, they are rare! They are rare! What a troupe we'll have! We'll bring down the house! We will make the balls *dance!*"

So the Apprentice Juggler lost his place in the troupe, but found another. For all who live by the rhythm of the inner timing, which the King approves, find a place in the Kingdom all their own. More than any, they live happily ever after.

Tales of the Kingdom, David and Karen Mains, David C. Cook, pages 29–30.

CHAPTER FOUR

LIVING IN DENIAL AND DELUSION

• Sometimes husbands or wives think, *If we just had the money the Rockefellers do, or the Kennedys, life would be so much easier.* But what happens with such a fortune is that you just inherit a new set of headaches. Wealthy families aren't any more problem-free than poor families.

DEALING WITH PROBLEMS
What's important for families is how they deal with their particular problems. According to Dolores Curran, author of the best-selling book, *Traits of a Healthy Family,* a healthy family *expects* problems and considers them to be a *normal* part of life.

In contrast, dysfunctional families are often marked by denial and delusion. They find their problems too painful to deal with so they just say, "There's really no problem here!"

Maybe the husband and father is an alcoholic, but that's too embarrassing for anyone to admit. The reality is just too hard to come to grips with. So the family pretends the problem doesn't exist. They live in a certain delusion, explaining away the obvious.

Perhaps the wife and mother is a workaholic. She's unable to be nurturing because she doesn't have any time for it. Her children have learned to go elsewhere when they need someone to talk to. That's because Mom always says something like, "Can't you see I'm busy at the moment, dear?" The project she's working on always takes priority. This mother's work is more important to her than her family's needs. "That's not true!" says Dad in her defense. "Your mom's a good person. You know that now, don't you? Someday maybe she won't be under so much pressure from work."

In reality that's wishful thinking. It's a denial of the truth.

In a healthy family, problems like this are confronted. Styles differ as to how they go about it. Some families visit a counselor or pastor. Or sometimes parents call a family conference where everyone has a say before a course of action is decided on.

Before moving on too quickly, let me just point out that within dysfunctional families this pattern of denial isn't as easy to recognize as one might think. An outside observer wonders how anyone could miss what's happening. But over time the family members have learned to look right past the obvious. They've gradually accepted the questionable behavior as normal . . . and excusable . . . and defensible.

Even when the problem has been pointed out by a professional counselor, it may take the family awhile to agree that, "Yes, Mom does have a work compulsion that's aberrant," or, "Dad needs to get help; his drinking isn't under control. Just because he still has his job doesn't prove anything." Patterns of denial are deep-rooted and families' defense systems can be incredibly creative.

There's a great deal of pain involved with denial. Sometimes it's felt immediately. For example, when Mom snaps, "I don't have time to talk right now; can't you see I'm under a great deal of pressure?" those words could actually bring tears to a child's eyes because of a strong sense of rejection.

Or, the pain of denial might be internalized, only to come out years later at unexpected times through intense anger or cursing or throwing tantrums. Why? Because a boss or friend or spouse or minister does something that reminds the adult child of what happened when he or she was young. And the person's not going to let that happen anymore. "So you're busy right now, and you can't see me for two days? You think you're so all fired important. Well, I'm important too! Forget you!"

Denial of problems in families doesn't make the pain go away. And the aftereffects can go on for decades.

Healthy families work toward the ideal of honesty in all their relationships. They don't want lies at the very center of their living. They declare, "If we have a problem, let's recognize it and work on it. If we need help, let's get it."

Throughout this book, I have been noting that often church families display the same symptoms as dysfunctional individual families. For example, sometimes church people don't understand that problems and conflicts are a normal part of congregational life. Because Jesus is present among believers, they assume that sanctification is instant. "If we're all converted, why can't we get along? We ought to just love each other. After all, one would think that the best family in the world should be problem-free!"

DENIAL OF SIN IN THE CHURCH

It's funny, isn't it? In the church, we know we're all sinners. The only problem is, nobody admits what his or her particular sin happens to be. In Alcoholics Anonymous meetings a person will say, "Hello, I'm William. I'm an alcoholic." That's the reality factor. But in church we don't say up front, "Hi, I'm David. I'm an addict. My problem is that I have an inordinate need for affirmation." Or, "I'm Betty. I tend to be a crybaby." Or, "I'm Ted. I have a problem with lust." Or, "I'm Jan. My tongue can get out of control if I'm not careful. But praise the Lord, I'm doing much better. Thanks for understanding and helping me become whole."

One of the problems with the contemporary church is that it's structured in such a way that openness and honesty are difficult to come by. When is it appropriate to say what you're struggling with? Do you do that during the worship hour? Hardly.

Do you write our your confession to be included in the Sunday bulletin?

Do you pick up an appropriate name tag in the church lobby and slap it on your dress or lapel? A tag that identifies your sin of greed, lying, gossip, or laziness?

What about confessing your sins during a Sunday School class? Do you just blurt out, "This last week I cheated on a test"? Or, "I was severely tempted to be dishonest at work." Or, "I'm a married man, and I made a pass at my company's receptionist."

My personal feeling is that the best forum for that kind of admission is established prayer partnerships. In that setting people have built a context for support and accountability and confidentiality. In a prayer partnership, Christians can feel comfortable sharing in all honesty.

I admit that the church doesn't put enough emphasis on prayer partnerships, but that could change.

ENCOURAGEMENT OF OPENNESS

The next best solution would be for small groups to take on the responsibility for encouraging openness. Churches are often lacking in the area of small groups as well. But we can change.

You see, when no forum has been provided to work through problems, sooner or later we get used to *pretending* we're OK. When trouble comes, everyone just acts shocked and says, "Such things should never be. What a pity."

But again, denial doesn't eliminate the pain. The hurt remains. Have you ever noticed that there are a lot of wounded people in our churches? Oh, you have, have you?

The Book of Ephesians is a letter written to a church. Chapter 4, verse 25, reads, "Therefore each of you must put off falsehood and speak truthfully to his neighbor, for we are all members of one body."

So here's a biblical emphasis on honesty. Again, healthy families (including healthy church families) work toward the ideal of honesty in all their relationships. They might not do it in the same way, but they figure out how to be open with one another because that's important.

How do we go about getting prayer partnerships — or small

groups—started through the church? First of all, keep in mind that dysfunctional family traits aren't changed overnight. They have been years—often generations—in the making. You don't just say a prayer and, "poof," they vanish.

That's true of dysfunctional *church* family traits too. We have to think of long-range results, of restructuring, of becoming more "New Testament." But we *can* do it.

The church is far better off today than it was twenty years ago. That's because of some hard thinking and a willingness to make changes on the part of people just like you. I say, let's keep at it.

And remember that for people to come to grips with denial involves their taking great risks. I know this from experience.

It's terrifying to think that your carefully built defenses might be dismantled, to realize that your rationale for the way you act is flawed. It's humiliating to acknowledge that the other person wasn't to blame in a given instance, that you were the one who behaved like a jerk. To face such a realization can be devastating. Should you open yourself to that possibility? Rather, if someone suggests that you're partially to blame for the breaches you have experienced in relationships, retaliate with a counterattack so powerful that the individual will know better than to ever say such a thing again.

The term *denial* is the professional counselors' way of referring to people's refusal to admit certain shortcomings or sins. Everyone else may recognize the lies, but not those in denial. They are insistent that their weaknesses don't exist. "I'm not impulsive in the way I act." "My drinking is under control." "Who's lazy?" "I don't hold grudges." "I don't know why you bring up procrastination, since that's not a serious problem for me." "Just because you say I'm a 'people pleaser' doesn't mean it's so."

I've come to believe that until a Christian is open to the voice of the Spirit, it doesn't matter who says what; he or she won't be able to hear it. The denial factor is just too great.

I couldn't hear that I was a workaholic. My wife said it for years, sometimes with tears, sometimes in anger. She bought me books to read about workaholism. Nothing changed. My defense system was practically foolproof.

Then one day at the dinner table I told my family that I felt the Lord was challenging me on the matter of how I treated my body. I wasn't exercising. I had gained weight. I drank way too much coffee. "I want you to help me, " I said. "Hold me accountable for change, OK?"

There was silence. My wife, my three sons, my daughter . . . none of them had known I was going to say what I did, that I would make a confession like this and ask for help. They were surprised that I introduced such a topic. So there was no collusion on their part.

"That's not your problem, Dad," said one of them finally. Then it was almost as if they were all speaking in unison. "If you want to overcome something significant, ask the Lord to help you stop being a workaholic. What you mentioned is not nearly as big a problem as this one, Dad. What you ought to be concerned about is that you work too much. When we wake up you're at the table working on a broadcast. Then you're gone all day, or you're out of town somewhere. And you still have your briefcase open at the table working when we go to bed."

I sputtered. I stammered. I tried to bring the conversation back around to what I had originally suggested. But this was a moment of truth. I could hear the hurt and the concern in what my children were saying. I saw the pain they felt because of my sin, because of my putting work above their needs. But I also sensed their love.

My defenses had been toppled. For the first time, I saw myself for who I was in this area. And I instantly knew that to try to rebuild my defense system would be dishonest and disobedient to what God was saying.

Well, that was just the beginning.

I've come a long way since then. I've learned a lot about why I'm addicted to work. I've memorized appropriate Scripture verses. I've gotten used to saying no to many of the ministry opportunities that come my way. I've "worked" at finding ways to relax. That's been hard, but it's coming.

TRANSFERRAL OF NEGATIVE PATTERNS

Part of my ongoing healing process has involved learning about dysfunctional families and how negative patterns are passed on from one generation to the next. Each new level of understanding has brought me closer to Christ's truth, and this is making me free. But the journey has certainly not been without pain and risk. Healing often involves a time of hurting, whether because of a surgeon's knife or the sword of the Spirit. How strong denial is and how difficult to overcome.

King David is a good example. When the Prophet Nathan approached him with a story of a rich man with a large number of sheep who took a ewe lamb from a poor man, David saw clearly the wrong that had been done. This ewe lamb was all the poor man had. It had grown up with him and his children. It shared his food, drank from his cup, and even slept in his arms. The ewe lamb was like a daughter to the poor man. But when a traveler came to the rich man he looked right past his flock and killed and served the visitor the poor man's ewe lamb. That made David angry. "He must pay for that lamb four times over," he decreed. "In fact, he deserves to die!"

"You're the man I'm talking about, David," said Nathan. "That is what you did with Uriah's wife, Bathsheba." And David experienced a moment of truth (see 2 Sam. 12).

Oh, how quickly those in denial make excuses—pass our blame on to others. It's as old as the events in Genesis 3. When God asked Adam and Eve, "Who told you that you were naked? Have you eaten from the tree I commanded you not to eat from?" the man quickly responded, "The woman you put here with me—she gave me some fruit from the tree" (vv. 11-12).

Eve acted the same way. She said, "The serpent deceived me" (v. 13). It's always the other person. *But we're still OK, God,* she thought, *nothing's wrong* . . . denial. It's always the other person. That's because admitting sin is very hard. But covering it up is to open your life to delusion. And denial and delusion are marks of dysfunctional families.

Obviously, no family is perfect. But a healthy family at least works toward the ideal of openness and honesty in all its relationships. When an individual or a family is coming to grips with denial, it's extremely important to do so in a safe environment.

If you're confronting denial in your life, you have to know you're loved. You need to be assured that nobody is going to shame you. The person dealing with you should be a long-time friend or cherished family member. Apparently, David could hear the Prophet Nathan; the integrity of the king's longtime companion was a great help in making him open to God's truth.

Just because Christ is present in His family, the church, doesn't mean we can expect people to be open about painful areas of their lives when they're in settings that haven't been established as "safety zones." Who knows what would happen if you stood during a Sunday morning worship service and said, "Please pray for me; I have a serious problem with greed (or with lust . . . or with jealousy)." That's not usually the right time or place for such an honest confession.

However, there are "safety zones" in congregations where prayer partnerships have been set up, where people get together in groups of two or three or even more, and pray together every week for several months. After feeling comfortable about the confidentiality that's been established, it's not unrealistic for someone to be able to say something like, "You know, I've been having a real struggle with my tongue. When I get angry I use crude words, and sometimes when I'm under pressure I take the Lord's name in vain. I really wish you'd pray for me."

Or, "I have a problem with another person. I've actually come to hate him, to hope he gets hurt, to wish him dead. I know this isn't right. Would you pray with me?"

Prayer partnerships are the right place for honest requests like those.

Maybe you're thinking, *I wish our church would set up prayer partnerships like that, but it hasn't.*

The truth is, you can do this on your own. You don't have

to wait for the church to organize prayer partnerships. Just think about who might be open to praying with you, someone you could trust. Approach the individual and decide what day and what time you could get together. Start making a list of things you might pray about — family, church, work, personal needs, friends who don't yet know Christ — and then try praying together a couple of times.

Don't start the first time together by dumping an emotional load on the other person. Allow the relationship to build, and then in time new levels of honesty will develop.

You see, we have to work at finding these safe places where total honesty can be experienced in the family of God. Otherwise, we force ourselves to live in denial and delusion. We end up with no place to go where we can be open, no haven from a world of painful delusion.

We need to work at creating that safe environment. It's not all-or-nothing, or, "If it doesn't work this first time, forget it!"

No, we construct these places of protection piece by piece. We build places where another person can eventually tell us, "It might be hard, but we'll walk through this together. I'll stick with you. Why? Because your friendship means a lot to me, that's why."

Isn't that what many of us need? And we have the ability to make it happen. I'm writing from experience. I have two close prayer relationships, and what places of comfort they have proved to be.

These prayer partnerships are not designed to be therapy sessions. I don't play the role of counselor when my friend shares a prayer request. I don't want him to do that for me either.

First I listen. Maybe I ask a question or two. Then I intercede on his behalf. In other words, I talk to the Lord about the concerns of my friend. He does the same on my behalf. If there's a counselor present it's the Holy Spirit.

But when we pray we believe God listens. And often He answers our prayers in marvelous and wonderfully creative ways. He makes us aware of His promise that where two or three gather in His name, the Lord Jesus is there as well. And eventually, He's the One who leads us into all truth. How wonderful.

Lord,
I praise You for Your truthfulness in dealing with people. You don't sweep problems under the rug, but You're always up-front and honest with us. You call us to be open with You as well, because You're intimately acquainted with all our thoughts, feelings, and concerns. Amen.

For Discussion and Reflection

1. Is the dysfunctional family trait of denial a new concept for you, or were you already familiar with it?

2. Has denial ever characterized you or your family? Are you open to talking about your experience?

3. Would you say that relationships in the church lean more toward denial or honesty? Why?

4. Describe a safe church setting where you would feel free to share honestly about how you are doing spiritually.

5. What do you suppose prohibits Christians from being more open in their relationships?

6. In an attempt to model honesty, how open should a pastor be about his own shortcomings? Under what circumstances might it be proper for him to talk about the temptations and victories of his parishioners?

READINGS

The drinking, incest, workaholism, drug dependency, mental illness, or codependency may be obvious to everyone else, but the family members simply refuse to admit anything is abnormal. To them the dysfunctional home *is* normal, even if miserable. Things that don't seem normal to the child at first—like daddy lying drunk in the front yard or mommy slumped in a chair dissolved in tears—are explained away as normal ("Daddy is camping" or "Mommy's stomach hurts"). Eventually the child doesn't trust his or her own perceptions anymore, and denial about how crazy things are becomes second nature.

But codependents don't just deny the reality of addiction or abuse. They also ignore the problems that come from dysfunction. The codependent compulsively engages in *magical thinking,* the unfounded expectation that the addiction-related difficulties will somehow improve by themselves—the alcoholic will quit drinking, the pornographer will throw away his books and tapes, the daughter will stop binging or start eating, the parent will begin spending less time at work and more time at home, the addicted wife will find a job and quit using, the husband will stop beating his wife and kids. Somehow the bills will be paid, the runaway will come home, the yard will get mowed, the spouse will become faithful, the children will no longer have problems at school, the broken bones will stop hurting. To maintain the illusion of normalcy, the codependent often must deny not only the primary prob-lem of addiction or abuse but also the secondary problems, both practical and relational, that flow out of the addiction or abuse.

There is a second level of denial that exists beneath the codependent's denial about family problems, both primary and secondary. In discussing this level of denial, Jael Greenleaf stated, "Concomitant with denial of the problem is denial of the feelings that the problems produce." This more basic level of denial involves repression, the refusal to allow oneself to feel the negative feelings associated with what's happening in the family.

From Bondage to Bonding, Nancy Groom, NavPress, pages 65–66.

■ ■ ■

But the subconscious mind can also be a tormenter, for it contains tremendous power for producing evil and misery. This especially relates to painful childhood memories. In trying to push them out of our minds, we actually bury them deeper and deeper, until they no longer can find a way out. As a result, the intense emotions we experienced but did not express, at the time the hurt occurred, have no way of being expressed now. Buried alive within our hearts, they retain amazing persistence and explosive power.

While we may think we are free of those apparently forgotten torments, this is not the case, for submerged memories cannot be stored away in peace in the same way that the mind files pleasant memories. Instead, we have to keep closing the door again and again, refusing to let these painful memories into our conscious minds. Since they can't enter through the door of our minds, they disguise themselves and try to smuggle into our personalities through another door.

The great effort required to keep these memories below the surface of the conscious mind is a constant drag on our energy. Some of us are as tired when we get up in the morning as when we went to bed at night, even though we have had eight hours of sleep. Why? All night long the battle has been raging in the depths of our personalities, causing a constant drain on our energies.

Many people live with the unresolved tensions of painful memories for years, during which the load increases. If such a person comes to the end of his endurance and finds his energies depleted, he becomes a prime candidate for an emotional crisis. If he is further weakened by physical exhaustion, illness, or traumatic shock, and then if some experience takes place which associates itself with a painful event of the past, those hidden memories he has so long tried to bury are awakened and reactivated.

When the dormant inner child of the past is thus aroused, he can take over the person's attitudes, reactions, outlook, and behavior. The submerged emotions rise up and express themselves in feelings of deep depression, rage, uncontrollable lust, inferiority, fear, loneliness, and rejection.

These painful memories are not automatically evicted or transformed by an experience of conversion or even by the filling of the Holy Spirit. They are not necessarily changed by growth in grace. In fact, these memories are often great hindrances to spiritual growth. And until a person receives deliverance from them, he does not really mature. It is as if one part of his person is in a deep freeze, or in a time machine. His body matures and his mind develops but that one particular area is still frozen. He remains a little boy, she is still a little girl, locked into that childhood stage of life.

Putting Away Childish Things, David A. Seamands, Victor Books, pages 18–20.

■ ■ ■

We do not know as well as we should like to know what the meetings of the first Christians were like in detail, but we have in the New Testament some extremely helpful indications. In any case we know enough to realize that these meetings were not at all what we think of as characteristic

Christian gatherings in our own day. The probability is that there was no human audience at all and not the slightest thought of a pattern in which one man is expected to be inspired to speak fifty-two times a year, while the rest are never so inspired. A clear indication of procedure is provided by Colossians 3:16 where we read "as you teach and admonish one another in all wisdom." The most reasonable picture which these words suggest is that of a group of modest Christians sitting in a circle in some simple room, sharing with one another their hopes, their failures, and their prayers. The key words are "one another." There are no mere observers or auditors; *all are involved.* Each is in the ministry; each needs the advice of the others; and each has something to say to the others. The picture of mutual admonition seems strange to modern man, but the strangeness is only a measure of *our* essential decline from something of amazing power.

The Company of the Committed, Elton Trueblood, Harper & Row, pages 31–32.

■ ■ ■

Sometimes when you read a story or see a film, you almost wish you were part of the action. It's more exciting than your everyday world. This may well be one of the additional surprises that comes from a prayer partnership. You begin to feel as though you're a part of the ongoing story of the expanding kingdom of Jesus Christ. You sense yourself living in the reality of the New Testament, being brothers and sisters with the apostles of old. This is really true! Numbers of people have made comments to us such as:

> "For the first time I see how I'm part of something bigger than just my own needs."
> "I never, ever remember hearing anyone pray for our denomination before. And the compassion in her voice convicted me of my indifference."
> "I've started reading some of the missionary mate-

rial I get in the mail. That's directly a result of my prayer partnership."

"The new person in our group had a list of ten people on what he called his "Most Wanted" list. These were non-Christians he was praying for. He thanked the Lord for one on his list who had just come to Christ. I felt convicted that I had never prayed for anyone like this."

"I never used the term 'miracle' before. But I heard my prayer partner ask the Lord for a miracle in this impossible situation. And it happened! All of a sudden I felt I was back in Bible times."

Many Christians who have been in prayer partnerships for long periods of time speak of the benefits that spill over into their relationships and responsibilities at church. One is the increasing comfort they feel about praying spontaneously with others. Before they were too intimidated, almost immobilized. They couldn't bring themselves to say to someone, "Why don't we pray about that right now?" Now they're experienced and confident enough to do it anytime.

In phone conversations they readily suggest, "Before we hang up, let me pray for you. Your need is legitimate. You have reason to be concerned. Let's take it to the Lord."

When someone at church asks for prayer, they don't just say, "I'll be praying for you," and let the matter drop. Rather, they respond, "Let's find a spot over there in the corner and I'll pray for you right now. That way you'll get a feel for how I promise I'll be praying for you during the days ahead."

Sometimes committee meetings or leadership meetings of the church are difficult. Typically they begin or end with prayer. But along the way, as hard issues arise, it can be good to have someone say, "Would you mind if we took a moment right now to pray about what's happening? I feel it would be more helpful for all of us if we could sense the presence of the Lord in this situation." Then after prayer, everyone present should be better able to hear Christ's voice in what is said. Wisdom to know the difference between what is good and what is best can emerge. As basic as it sounds, the insertion of prayer can often be the most effective way to find solutions to difficult situations.

Is it being too bold or too pushy to suggest to people who have mentioned a prayer request, "Let's stop right now and pray about that matter"? Might some people resent being prayed for on the spot? The answer is almost always "no!" In fact, both of us can point to numerous times when we prayed for someone and looked up to see tears in the person's eyes. Each of us has heard comments like, "Thank you so much. I've never had anyone do that for me before. You can't imagine what an encouragement your interest in my problem is. I'm deeply touched that you actually took the time to pray with me." Other times no words were spoken, but an embrace, a spontaneous gesture of gratitude, said volumes.

What we're reporting isn't unique to us. Many believers have experienced what we're describing. You may be one who could describe similar incidents. If not, would you like to be such a person? Does this kind of ministry—encouraging those who are hurting and in need—sound attractive to you? It's not that complicated to bring hope to someone through prayer. *Getting involved in a prayer partnership and staying with it trains you to be such a person.*

Two Are Better Than One, David Mains and Steve Bell, Multnomah, pages 45–49.

■ ■ ■

"I have some things I want to work on over the next several weeks. And, frankly, I find that everytime I'm around you I leave realizing that you've taught me something—even when you don't say much. What hour of the week might work best for getting together? I'd like to pull in a couple of other guys too. What would you think of that?"

How would you respond to such a phone call? Look at what the proposal suggests:

1. A one-hour weekly meeting.
2. Intentional agenda—"some things."

3. A group of up to four men.

4. Voluntary participation.

5. Sustained time—"the next several weeks."

Many men are dying on the vine and would leap at the opportunity for an intentional support group. Think of what they face: career decisions, marital questions, parenting problems, coping with the seductions of culture, job frustration, and deeper personal integrity issues.

Men meet in bars, tell stories, make confessions, laugh and cry, bump, slap, and hug each other—all gestures denoting deep needs to establish relationships with others. Men hunt, fish, play golf, watch television sports, and go to service club luncheons and prayer breakfasts together. But what characterizes most of these contacts is their superficiality. It has been my experience that "intentional agenda" is the missing ingredient in most of these group experiences.

But for every man who goes to the Rotary, Silver Bullet, or prayer breakfast, there are likely ten more who move like zombies through their daily and weekend routine. Many resort to the weekend anesthesia of *Michelob,* and only deepen their isolation from wife and children. If any group of men needs intentional agenda accountability with peers, it is these men who drop more deeply into the isolated and lonely male syndrome. Often these men reduce themselves, almost systematically, to a robotic wasteland of punching time clocks, performing jobs, picking up checks, then checking out of the human race until Monday morning.

Do you find yourself in such a rut? If so, let me challenge you to respond to the following questions:

1. Who might share my need for accountability and support?

2. What immediate questions would I be willing to risk airing with some peers?

3. What time and plan might work?

Are you serious about resolving the unfinished business in your life? Then after answering these questions, get ready to make your first phone call.

Unfinished Business, Donald Joy, Victor Books, pages 180–182.

CHAPTER FIVE

COMPULSIVE/ ADDICTIVE BEHAVIOR

• An addict is a slave to his habit. The word comes from the Latin *addictus* which in Roman law meant a debtor awarded as a slave to his creditor.

Today we read a lot about the new "creditors" to which people have become debtors. For example, millions in North America are slaves to alcohol. The same is true in regard to drugs. Smoking is another major addiction.

There are workaholics and ragealcoholics, as well as people controlled by gambling or sex. A "couch potato" is someone in the process of becoming a slave to television. Certain people can't stop eating, and others can't stop spending.

It's easy to come up with a list of addictions like this. But if I mention them too quickly, I do an injustice to the families where these are real problems. Their pain is so great that the least we can do is attempt to feel what for them is an ongoing nightmare.

THE HOPELESSNESS OF ADDICTION

We need to pause to observe the head of a household coming home drunk time after time. His slurred words are crude and his actions abusive. See the fear in the eyes of his wife and children.

Or sense the great sadness of parents whose son or daugh-

ter is hooked on drugs. You can almost touch their hopelessness. They're battling a monster they don't know how to
fight. You wish you could help but you too realize the problem is overwhelming.

Visit someone in the final stages of emphysema or lung
cancer. You know this person deserves a longer life and a
more dignified death. And you don't argue with the spouse
who strongly wishes cigarettes were banned.

See the tears accompanying the deep feelings of abandon-
ment common to those who live with a workaholic.

Would anyone say that gambling is a friend of the family, or
that pornographic magazines, books, or films serve a family
well?

That's enough. I just wanted to be sure we were in touch
with the real pain caused by this next characteristic of dysfunctional families—compulsive/addictive behaviors.

Sometimes it's not easy to differentiate between those two
terms. But in my thinking it helps to see addictions in the
context of a person's being a slave to something. His or her
master is drugs, food, work, sex, anger, smoking, watching
television, gambling, or spending. The individual is controlled
by such a master and submits to its will.

COMPULSIVE BEHAVIOR

By contrast, compulsive behavior is more in the realm of an
irresistible impulse to perform irrational acts. For example, a
person can become compulsive about hand-washing or cleaning the house time and again, or making lists. There's nothing wrong with washing one's hands or cleaning the house or
making lists unless these things are done all the time. In the
same way there's nothing wrong with talking unless someone
can't stop talking, which means the person is a compulsive
talker. Know anyone like that?

Compulsive behavior is probably not as serious as addictive
patterns, but sometimes the two categories sort of nudge up
against each other.

As with addictions, compulsive behavior has a frustration
factor that can open the door to hurt. Someone who is a

compulsive complainer, who finds fault with everyone, who becomes an expert at spotting the flaws in others—after awhile such a person can drive everyone nuts, even those in his or her immediate family. The same is true of a compulsive talker or cleaner or list-maker.

How can we tell the difference between what's a bad habit and a compulsive pattern? I can't draw neat lines for you. But often what begins as a bad habit eventually becomes compulsive and/or addictive behavior.

Maybe the practice of having a cigarette now and then, or a drink every so often, ultimately becomes an addiction. Or what begins as a bad habit of occasionally being late, in time becomes a compulsive behavior. Now the person *always* arrives twenty minutes to an hour late. I've read that Marilyn Monroe was compulsive in this sense, regularly being several hours late for important film shoots.

It's not infrequent that in dysfunctional families such flaws are passed on from one generation to the next. The addiction to rage, sex, eating disorders, workaholism is replicated.

Remember the biblical accounts of Abraham's habit of lying about his wife when they traveled in unfamiliar settings? It happened twice. Sarah was beautiful, and Abraham feared he would be killed so that she could be taken as a wife by another man. So Abraham said Sarah was his sister. He may have thought this would preserve his life, but this habit certainly left Sarah vulnerable.

Abraham's son, Isaac, copied his father's pattern exactly. Lies also marked the lives of Isaac's twin sons, Jacob and Esau. And would you believe this lack of truth-telling also characterized Jacob's sons, who broke his heart by telling him Joseph had been killed by a wild animal, when in fact they had sold him into slavery. How many times this intergenerational pattern of passing on sins is repeated.

COMPULSIVE/ADDICTIVE PEOPLE
IN THE CHURCH

Unfortunately, when compulsive/addictive people become a part of the church family, they bring to it the same problems they have in their own families. Those people who have trouble getting to school or work on time have an even greater problem arriving at church on time. They're always late. In years to come their children will probably be late too. And most likely, so will their grandchildren.

Look out if a man who is compulsive about neatness is asked to serve on the church maintenance committee. He will no doubt begin to see the church as his building to protect and keep immaculate. It doesn't matter that others see the facility as something to be used, not a museum.

The person who chronically "bad-mouths" people will not know when to quit, whether he or she is talking about the pastor, the music director, the youth leader, or a person serving on the same committee.

The family that habitually sits in the same pew might be unexpectedly upset when they find it occupied by visitors.

The man or woman addicted to "religious highs" will be thrilled or disappointed depending on who preaches, or who sings, or who gives a testimony.

The individual who is a slave to gossip will bring that addiction from home right into the church—unless a major healing occurs.

The compulsive need to control will mark a person whether at work during the day or at a church board meeting in the evening.

Compulsive/addictive behavior doesn't magically vanish when one drives onto the church parking lot. So the church needs to become skilled at graciously helping "slaves" gain their freedom from the chains of compulsive/addictive behavior.

In Ephesians 5, Paul discusses those kinds of problems. He writes (v. 3): "But among you there must not be even a hint of sexual immorality, or of any kind of impurity, or of greed, because these are improper for God's holy people."

Then Paul adds (vv. 8, 11-14b):

For you were once darkness, but now you are light in the Lord. . . . Have nothing to do with the fruitless

deeds of darkness, but rather expose them. For it is
shameful even to mention what the disobedient do in
secret. But everything exposed by the light becomes
visible, for it is light that makes everything visible.

So the church must play the role of making sure that lies at
the center of members' lives aren't allowed to remain unex-
posed. Christ's truth is to control all that they do. His light is
meant to expose these dark places.

But be aware that from the very beginning, people have
always been afraid of this divine light. Often part of the darkness has been a central characteristic of their family system.
They're highly threatened to think this trait might be revealed by a divine spotlight. So the corrective work must be
done in as kind a fashion as possible. But it has to be done.
Otherwise, when flawed and hurting people come to church,
they in turn can hurt others. That's just the way it is.

So the Spirit of Christ, who is alive in His children, will
always work at shining His light on sin. Personal areas of
darkness must be exposed for the sake of the individual, yes,
but also for the sake of the well-being of the family.

All Christians must have an intense desire to become more
and more characterized as children of the light. You see,
children of the light don't adversely influence the church
through bad habits, compulsive behavior, or addictions.

So in spite of a family history of negative patterns, "Jacobs" in the church must stop being grabbers in order to
become princes with God, men and women who prevail in
spiritual matters.

As destructive as it was to allow the enslavement of Afri-
cans to mark the church in earlier generations, so in our day
we must see different kinds of slaves set free.

Remember that families don't change unless individuals
within families do. And church families improve only as nu-
clear families and individual members of the church get
better.

Fortunately, when there's a spiritual breakthrough in one
person's life, it normally has a positive effect on others. So

the question of how a church changes is not that different from asking how individuals change.

In this regard the New Testament writers see certain lessons as obvious. John, for example, writes that "God is light; in Him there is no darkness at all. If we claim to have fellowship with Him yet walk in the darkness, we lie and do not live by the truth" (1 John 1:5-6).

Paul writes almost the same thing in Ephesians. "Live as children of light (for the fruit of the light consists in all goodness, righteousness and truth) and find out what pleases the Lord" (Eph. 5:8-10).

Light and darkness, truth and lies, good and evil—usually it's not hard to distinguish between these opposites.

The writer to the Hebrews chides his readers, "In fact, though by this time you ought to be teachers, you need someone to teach you the elementary truths of God's Word all over again. You need milk, not solid food! . . . Solid food is for the mature, who by constant use have trained themselves to distinguish good from evil" (Heb. 5:12, 14).

"The acts of the sinful nature are obvious," writes Paul in Galatians 5:19. And he lists specific addictions like sexual immorality, witchcraft, hatred, jealousy, fits of rage, drunkenness, and orgies. Paul's right—these are obviously not of God.

"But," he continues, "the fruit of the Spirit is love, joy, peace . . . kindness . . . self-control" (vv. 22-23). You know the list. Then Paul challenges us, "Since we live by the Spirit, let us keep in step with the Spirit" (v. 25). I'll return to that phrase.

The point is, it's not hard to understand these things. So when bad habits, compulsive patterns, or addictions mark people of the church, it shouldn't take Christians forever to figure out whether this is fitting behavior.

Maybe some compulsions or addictions are a bit tricky, as in the case of the man who feels compelled to say yes whenever he's asked to serve. He always says yes whether or not he has the time or the talents.

Or what about the woman who has her Christian radio

station on all day, watches religious television regularly, and shows up whenever there's a meeting at church. She's a religion addict. But even matters like these become obvious as time goes on.

"So, Lord, shine Your light on me." That's what we need to be praying. "I give You permission to do this. In fact, I encourage You to. Don't let any lies remain at or around the center of my life. I want to be marked by what Paul calls goodness, righteousness, and truth. Amen."

Now this request differs from personal introspection. It's not morbid self-examination, but rather a straightforward and expectant prayer. It simply says, "If there are areas of darkness in me, Lord, I want You to expose them by Your divine light. Do that for my sake, and also for the good it will bring to others in Your family of faith."

And God answers that prayer—through your conscience, through special insight He gives you, through His Word, through a book you read or a conference you attend, through a sermon or broadcast you hear, through a comment of a friend, through any of an infinite number of ways. And because of your prayer, instead of resisting His work you welcome it.

If criticism comes your way you ask God, "Were You speaking to me through what this person said?" Then in your quiet time alone with Him, you're usually able to discern whether the critical remark was a word from the Lord. If you're not sure, just tell the Lord, "I'm confused on this one. I'm going to put things on hold and wait for further clarification."

I believe this is part of what Paul is referring to when he talks about keeping in step with the Spirit.

KEEPING IN STEP WITH THE SPIRIT

When you were in school, did you ever play in a marching band? If so, perhaps the band did formations during halftime at football games. Or maybe you marched together in the annual Memorial Day parade.

If my memory is accurate, our Quincy High marching band

in southern Illinois was about a hundred members strong. I played baritone and was in row two at the extreme left.

In my mind, parades were worse than halftime shows, because in a parade we might follow a group of horses. Then we had other things to concentrate on besides the music or whether our line was straight!

Our band was good. When we marched our ranks were precise and our music was terrific. Our director made sure of it. He took a lot of pride in how we did.

But have you ever seen a band where the whole unit turned a corner except for one trombone player who kept going straight? Or a band that looked pretty good except for several members who were obviously out of step? Or a group whose ranks were wavy as they passed by? Or whose music wasn't solid or together? Or a band where somebody missed the warning and stepped in the filth left by the horses in front!

Good marching bands know how to stay in step. When Paul writes about keeping in step with the Spirit, he's talking about groups as well as individuals. His letter to the Galatians was written to several churches in the region. So his challenge is plural — "Since *we* live by the Spirit, let *us* keep in step with the Spirit." So this is a word to individuals, but also to churches. And it's very graphic, isn't it?

I recall hearing this text unfolded by Colonel Eric Britcher of the Salvation Army. Appropriately enough, he picked up on the marching band imagery. His message has stuck in my mind since then. How marvelous it would be to behold a church passing by whose members all "Keep in step with the Spirit of Christ." Or to get even closer to the original meaning, "Keep on keeping in step with the Spirit."

It will take a few at the start to catch the vision, to set the example, to say, "We can do it! Come on." Then others will respond.

Yes, to keep in step with the Spirit, some bad habits will have to be overcome. We can't walk in the darkness. Some compulsions will need to be challenged. We can't be bound by the fear of what others might think. That's an addiction. Instead, we'll concentrate on what God thinks. Are we doing what pleases Him?

And before long there will be a noticeable change. Because of better cooperation the messes we used to get into will be avoided. The ranks will be straighter then and the music sounding better. There will be a healthy sense of pride in the unit. Others will want to join up. The director's wishes will be honored, and we'll keep on keeping in step with the Spirit.

Those watching will applaud. They know what they expect of us, and they'll appreciate it when those expectations are met.

I look forward to a day in the near future when church after church parades by the reviewing stand, and they are terrific. I picture the Nazarenes, the Methodists, the Lutherans, the Baptists, the Assemblies—all with their unique touches—but everyone marked by true class. "Keep on keeping in step!"

Black church bands playing soul music. Asian, Hispanic, and white church bands all sounding different and wonderful. Suburban congregations, small town and farm community bands, and city bands. As we know national revival, they too will keep in step with the Spirit. Lord, give us another of those days in the church when we hear "Seventy-six trombones led the big parade."

But for such a time to come, all of us must determine to do our part to keep in step with the Spirit. That means adjustments must be made in my life, and probably in yours.

These changes involve putting aside bad habits. We need to be open to the Spirit's challenge regarding compulsive behavior that's detrimental to the overall well-being of the family of God. And keeping in step with the Spirit means our renouncing addictions, like my addiction to work—addictions that are deeply ingrained.

But I feel the vision is attractive enough for me to say, "Change me, Lord. Go ahead, do it!" I want to be part of a church generation that knows how to march with some of the great bands of the past.

What needs to happen is that through the Spirit of Christ, believers are set free from bad habits, compulsive behavior, and even addictions. When this freedom begins to express itself, it signals a great new day for the best family in the world—even a day of revival in the church.

Lord,
I praise You for Your power to make all things new. You call us to break free from compulsive patterns that inhibit or control us, so that we can enjoy the wholeness You offer. Thank You for often surprising us by the creative ways You bring healing to our lives. Amen.

For Discussion and Reflection

1. Name some compulsive/addictive behaviors you have seen new Christians bring with them to the church.

2. What specific negative habits in the church have you observed being handed down from one family generation to another?

3. When have you been challenged to move forward spiritually because of the progress being made by someone else in your congregation?

4. What examples can you recall of people giving God permission to shine His light on their sins?

5. When you're criticized by someone, how can you tell whether the Lord is trying to say something to you through that person?

6. How good is your church at "keeping on keeping in step with the Spirit"?

READINGS

Addiction has been described in many ways. It has been called a disease, a moral weakness, lack of willpower, and sin. While there is an element of truth to each of these ideas, the point for right now is that addiction is a process. Addiction seldom remains constant. As it changes, it usually takes more and more of a person's energy and resources, to the point that it can become destructive and even fatal. Addiction is a set of experiences that produces changes within the person. The addict, responding to these internal changes, will begin to act out in particular ways. As addiction develops, it becomes a way of life. Since there are common patterns in this progression, we can use these characteristics to serve as bench marks of the addictive process.

To understand addiction we need to remember something very basic about human nature. We tend to want to do things that are rewarding and positive, and we tend to avoid things which are negative and aversive. If it hurts, we try to stop the pain. If it feels good, we want to do it again. If the conditions of the Garden of Eden were still in effect, there would be no addiction. The reason? Because there would be continual contentment, and no beginning for pain.

However, we live in a world where there are cycles of feeling. We desire to feel happy and to experience peace of mind. Sometimes we are able to experience pleasure. But it can't last forever. Life is not a constant mountaintop existence. The good feelings seem to slip away. When they leave, we may grieve, feel sad, or become depressed over the loss. On the other hand, it is just as inevitable that pain, hurt, or other negative experiences will enter our lives. It is inevitable that we will lose a loved one, suffer a loss of status, have a dream or ideal shattered, experience an end of a friendship, or have a prayer that seems unanswered in the way we want. These are the times when a person is susceptible to forming an addictive relationship.

Because we want to escape pain, we seek out objects or experiences that maximize the positive and eliminate the negative. There is a certain element of control we can exert in helping these cycles along, but the ups and downs are unavoidable. Since we cannot totally control the cycle of peace and pain, we must learn to either accept these cycles or try to be happy all of the time. The addict tries to control these uncontrollable events. When he engages in a particular object or event to produce a desired mood change, he believes he can control the cycle. The addict believes he can make the pain go away and bring about good feelings whenever he wants. And in the beginning he can be successful. But this is where the process becomes progressive. Just as cancer is a process involving the uncontrolled multiplying of harmful cells, addiction is the out-of-control search for either happiness or the avoidance of pain. Regardless of the addiction, every addict has a relationship with an object or event in order to produce a mood change.

When Good Things Become Addictions, Grant Martin, Victor Books, pages 10–11.

■　■　■

The toxic faith system is all too willing to have religious addicts join because it is created to take advantage of those who seek escape rather than faith. They escape into the accepting arms of those who want to see more and more new recruits. They escape into an unreal world where people, ideas, and rules replace a relationship with God. The farther they drift from God, the more desperate the addicts become, until they are willing to lie, cheat, steal, or kill for the toxic faith organization or its leader. They become so hooked that they are almost unreachable or unapproachable because their denial is so strong. They hit bottom and change, go crazy, or kill themselves. Those are the only three alternatives for religious addicts who have progressed through all of the addictive stages.

Religious addiction doesn't occur overnight. It is a long progression that subtly captures every aspect of the addict's life. It rarely begins in adulthood. Most of the time the roots of addiction can be traced back to a difficult childhood. In the early years the seeds of toxic faith are planted that eventually grow into an addiction. Those seeds can be anything from rigid parenting to ritual abuse involving children in the occult. Whatever the source of the toxic faith seeds, the future addict is on a course in search of a god that does not exist, a god that is a creation of man, like any other idol created in our own image.

Just as a foundation is laid, it can be ripped up. No one is doomed to a life of religious addiction and toxic faith. If a person is willing to go through the painful process of breaking through the denial and seeing the addictive progression, there is hope for change.

Toxic Faith, Stephen Arterburn and Jack Felton, Oliver Nelson, pages 126–127.

■ ■ ■

"I walked across a patch of bare ground upon which a shanty town had recently stood"; writes James [an investment banker about the Well, a ministry for addicts in Hong King's walled city]. "In a final glance, I saw the gleaming office skyscrapers, the resettlement blocks, the airport, and the lion-shaped rock on the hill-top which provided the backdrop, and contrast, to the Walled City. I could not see, even from fifty yards away how to get into it.

"The passageway, one of the primary arteries, was about four feet wide. It was almost dark inside. I could not look down because of the open watercourse running along the middle of the passage, covering half its width and carrying fetid, smelly and swirling water. In amongst the rubbish and filth on either side, rats did not even bother me as I passed. I could not look up either, because at about eye level (for me) ran the illegal water pipes and electricity cables; years of rubbish thrown down from above, mixed with the dripping pipes and the rain, had formed these into a dense and matted ceiling with the consistency of the underlie of a cheap hotel bath plug.

"I hurried along, hunch-shouldered and crying. Some of those who helped at the Well said that they had cried when they went in. It helps a bit. To the right, a central hand pump with fifteen to twenty people washing themselves and their clothes. No smiles here, no laughter. To the left, the clattering, unimaginable clattering of a metal rolling machine in a tiny factory. Shadowy figures, no laughter.

"Somewhere in the middle was the Well, a green room, bright, with a fan, scrubbed clean. An addict, the remains of a man, was squatting outside the door, steeling himself to go in. There were about thirty like him inside, a few Western helpers and some of the Chinese brothers, ex-addicts and now helpers, whose testimonies three years earlier had forced me to reconsider Jesus, and my whole way of life.

"Each addict, skinny, grey, drawn, was prayed for when he came in. Some received then and there the strength to face the task of starting again and the certainty that their withdrawal would not involve pain. For others this came in the next one or two visits.

"I saw the helpers explaining that, by praying, any such symptoms would disappear, even before they were evident. Times without number over the following six weeks I was to see and participate in moments when this occurred. It does not just involve seeing a man's eyes change from hopelessness and desperation to peacefulness, but an entire change in the way he holds himself; creases of pain go, shoulders square, a smile appears. Laughter comes. It was extremely challenging at the outset, but quickly became immensely humbling, immensely exciting as I watched the Lord at work.

"After a time of prayer, a time of worship followed at the meeting. The atmosphere was charged as we sat or stood in a circle round the guitars. One of the addicts, new to the Well, passed on aloud the answer to the unspoken fear of many there who had never received anything for nothing: 'So, you think you have nothing to give me? Give me your pain, give me your suffering, give me your fear, and I will give you life.' The effect was explosive, a great release of things held back, kept down, shut away. They cried, they shouted, they sang, they laughed. So did I.

"On my return three months later, I saw some of those I had first encountered at the Well. Brown, stronger, fatter, wreathed in smiles. It took me a while to recognize who they had been."

Crack in the Wall, Jackie Pullinger, Hodder & Stoughton, pages 43–44.

■ ■ ■

"All my life," he said, "I have been dominated by hatred. My stepfather never cared for me, I was always beaten. He beat my mother too and when I saw her lying crushed on the floor I was sick to my stomach. But she never loved me. She hated me and treated me as a burden. By the time I was a man, I had so much hatred. I never knew love. I started killing people and at first it was hard. But once you kill one person you can go on forever. There is so much guilt, you cannot stop. You cannot admit that you hate yourself, and that you have done this terrible thing."

The Nubian spoke so intensely that sweat began dripping from his face. *I am looking at a man who has come to his end,* I thought to myself. *He has no more mental or emotional strength.* . . .

"When we came to kill you Easter morning," he said, "we were going to kill you in front of everyone. We were going to show you our power. But we kept sitting in the service. I didn't hear anything you said, I could only see the widows and orphans who were sitting around me. Some of them I knew. I had killed their men with my own hands, and I expected them to be weeping and mourning. But they were clapping, they were singing songs and they were happy. Their joy made me so afraid. I thought to myself, if for one moment I could understand it, I would give up everything.

"When we came to this room and you prayed for us, I did understand. I felt something in my life I had never felt before. But now I have read of this man Jesus. And I cannot believe. I cannot be forgiven. My father is Satan. Every night I go to bed and see the faces of the people I have killed. I hear their screams and the screams of their women and children. I never heard them before, but now I hear nothing else. They never leave my heart and I cannot be forgiven."

As I listened to him pour out his torment, my fear for my own life completely disappeared. I wanted to comfort him, to convince him of God's forgiveness but I could find no words to speak. For a moment I myself even doubted that God would want to forgive such a man. How much human misery he had brought to our lives! How many people he had destroyed! I thought of the Okelo family and their bloodstained living room. Perhaps this man had been the one who tortured and tore them limb from limb.

With a great effort I pushed these thoughts aside and picked up my Bible. In the past months my own speech had often failed me but the words of Scripture had been life and truth. Now I read with the Nubian testimony after testimony of God's love and forgiveness. When we had finished, the words of Isaiah had become a new and living reality for us both:

I have blotted out, as a thick cloud, thy transgressions, and, as a cloud, thy sins; return unto me; for I have redeemed thee.

The Nubian prayed that God would continue to reveal to him the truth of His Word and together we asked God to empow-

er us by the Holy Spirit, that we might believe in the forgiveness of sins.

On the following Sunday I saw the Nubian again. He and
the four men who had invaded the church vestry were now
attending our church services and afterwards he came alone
to meet me in the vestry. His face was covered with a broad
smile and he moved as if he were about to dance.

"I have found the love of Jesus Christ," he said. "I am a
new man. I can feel it, my sins have been taken away. A few
days ago I was ordered on a raiding mission by my commander. When we came to the house we were supposed to plun-
der, I pointed my gun in the face of the owner and he was
trembling. Then I told him, 'You are a lucky man. If I had met
you two weeks ago you would be a dead man. But I have met
Jesus Christ and my sins have been forgiven. I am a free man
and I will free you.' Then I let him go."

I was so happy to see the transformation in the Nubian's
life that I hardly noticed his strange method of evangelism.
Later, when it came to mind, I did not know whether to laugh
or to sigh. Testifying from behind a loaded gun! The chaos of
Amin's regime was certainly producing bizarre testimonies.

From this man I learned anew that the blood of Jesus
Christ covers a multitude of sins. The Nubian was a man
whose life had been shaped by the absence of God's love.
From the beginning he had been a rejected personality, a man
who hated his own image. He had tried to recapture his
human dignity by destroying other human beings, but he had
only fallen deeper into self-hatred and insecurity. It was a
vicious circle: the more he hated himself the more cruelly he
acted, and the more cruelly he acted the more he hated himself. But now, by the love of Jesus Christ, he had been released from this bondage. He had a new and secure identity
as a child of God.

I thought of Idi Amin. His father had left him at birth and
his mother had toured army barracks as a camp prostitute.
His tribe, the Sudanese Nubians, had become notorious for
their sadistic brutality and vengeful spirits. Perhaps Amin too
was a man who had never known God's love. Perhaps he too

found his self-worth only in hating. If so, his insecurity could only become paranoia. Hundreds of thousands of people had died by his hand and at the hands of his Nubian mercenaries. In a society of extended families, where one death means two hundred enemies, such crimes were unforgivable. Amin's enemies were innumerable, and the more he tried to eliminate them, the more new enemies he made. He too was caught in a vicious cycle.

A Distant Grief, F. Kefa Sempangi, Regal, pages 126–129.

■ ■ ■

Now the Holy Spirit immediately takes over the new believer's conscience on conversion. Before, it was basically programmed by the norms of society. But now a new force begins to make itself known. It's almost as though Jesus Himself were present with you, saying, "Oh, oh, I'd stay away from that if I were you. Over here is something good you might want to try." If you were to obey Christ in everything He said, you would soon be quite a disciple, a student of this teacher, which is what the word disciple means. In similar fashion, if you always respond to the Holy Spirit, who's taken Christ's place as He brings things to your conscience, you'll grow just like the people you read about in the Bible.

"But how do I know it's the Holy Spirit and not the devil?" you ask. "Can't he put thoughts in my mind, too?"

Certainly, but frankly, very seldom is it that hard to tell the difference. Maybe it would help just to clarify the names by which this new Counselor is called. First he is the *Holy* Spirit. So when it's a matter of holiness, it's a message from God. He's also very appropriately named the Spirit of *truth.* You'll find him hammering away at this until not only are outright lies taboo, but also any slanting or shading or exaggerating of the facts. Spiritual children know when they should respond to God regarding their naughty tongues, and certainly there's no real question as to the source of the promptings.

Scripture speaks about the *love* of the Spirit. A strong impulse to do a good thing on another's behalf should be seen as having been initiated by God. Regularly, the Bible refers to the Holy Spirit as the Spirit of *Jesus,* or of *Christ.* Again, any inner encouragement to act in a Christlike manner need not be questioned. Numerous other names could be mentioned, but these are enough to make the point.

Unfortunately, I fear most believers treat the ministry of the Spirit too lightly. Dr. David McKenna tells about the troubled soul who went for professional help.

"What's your problem?" the counselor queried.

"Well, you see, I don't have the will power to resist temptation, and my conscience is uneasy."

"Then you would like to strengthen your will power, is that right?"

The patient paused, dropped his head, and then answered sheepishly, "Well, not exactly. If it's all right with you, sir, I'd prefer to have my conscience weakened!"

Getting to Know the Holy Spirit, David R. Mains, David C. Cook, pages 29–30.

CHAPTER SIX

PERFECTIONISM

• Church-hoppers jump from one congregation to another. Many of them are looking for the perfect place to worship. They'll never find it!

That's because no church is perfect. No pastor is. No program is. No congregation of believers is. Look all their lives if they want, these church-hoppers won't find that elusive place.

Maybe what they should search for instead is a church with no more problems than they can tolerate, and hopefully one where the leaders are consistently adequate.

But already I'm writing about the church when I should have begun with the family. My pattern has been to point out various traits of dysfunctional families and then show how these negative characteristics often infiltrate the family of God.

APPEARANCE MANAGEMENT

Perfectionism is a major problem in many unhealthy families. Everything has to appear exactly right. When a problem surfaces in a home like this, parents concern themselves with "appearance management." How do we cover over this situation so we'll look OK? After all, what will our friends and neighbors think? What might someone at the church say?

"Now listen, all of you, don't you breathe a word of this problem outside this house, do you hear me?"

A family taken up with appearances can't allow room for mistakes. But what a burden this is, to feel they have to look perfect, to act perfect, to live with the illusion of perfection.

If a young daughter gets pregnant, keep acting like all's well. Do what you must to make things appear right. What's best for her isn't the important thing. The priority is keeping up the pretense that "everything's fine with us, thank you for asking."

But how awful to have to pretend. And how painful to have to live up to such impossible expectations. If the standard is set at 100 percent, the best batters in baseball are miserable failures, because they only get a hit about every three times at bat. Good basketball teams often miss as many shots as they take. In spite of the fact that many football plays are designed to score a touchdown, very few of them actually do. In these performance-oriented worlds participants have learned to be satisfied with being consistently adequate— with getting the job done and viewing the spectacular achievements as added blessings.

CONSISTENT ADEQUACY

That's what parents in healthy families are satisfied with— being consistently adequate. Then they're surprised and pleased when things go better than expected.

What a freeing term this is—"consistently adequate." (I am indebted to Dr. Sandra Wilson for this freeing concept. See her book *Released from Shame.*) Raising a healthy family is not an easy task. But certainly the inevitable problems faced by families today are handled more easily when they don't have to worry about being perfect.

The same is true when it comes to the family of God. Pastors can't always preach sermons that are "tens." But how wonderful if they're consistently adequate. If a few "tens" get tossed into the Sunday morning mix every so often, better yet!

Your dozen or so singers won't rival the sounds of the

Mormon Tabernacle Choir. But are they consistently adequate in the way they express praise to the Lord on behalf of your church body?

So what if the children's Sunday School program isn't better than a weekly one-hour trip to Disneyland. Is it consistently adequate? If it is, be grateful.

All churches (like all families) have problems. When these come up, and they inevitably will, it's a lot easier to deal with them if God's people aren't worried about trying to appear perfect.

Isn't problem-solving a lot of what churches are all about? God help us if the bottom line is appearance management.

Church families caught up with appearances can easily end up being performance-oriented. If a child cries in the service the preacher gets upset. If the soloist forgets some words or flats a note, someone complains. After a while the worship ends up being more like a television production than a place for people to come and have their needs met, or to praise the Lord to the best of their ability, or to find encouragement to go out and face their everyday world.

A woman told me recently (with tears) how she hadn't been to church for a number of years. Her husband refused to go, so she hadn't been attending either. But she felt such a need for God. So one Sunday morning, with some effort, she got herself and her two small children ready and took them with her to a church she had heard good things about. It was a twenty-minute drive, but what difference does that make when you're looking for God? When she arrived, however, she was told that children as young as hers were not allowed in the service. They might disturb someone. She assured the usher they were well-behaved, but that didn't matter. So she took them to children's church. But both of them were reluctant to be left without their mother in these new surroundings. So eventually the woman just went back home—greatly embarrassed and distressed. And it was another two years before she tried attending a church service again.

Don't misunderstand, I'm not for noisy services, bad sermons, poorly rehearsed choir numbers, or for last-minute, thrown-together Sunday School lessons. I'm just saying that the bottom line can't be, "Do we look good?" Because that's not what ministry is all about.

It's great when churches are skilled at ministry and also do things with excellence. I applaud them. May their kind increase.

And I applaud the far larger number of churches that are skilled at ministry and consistently adequate in all they do. May their kind also increase.

MINISTRY

Ministry has to do with reaching out to people who feel as if they don't belong. It's saying, "There's a place here for you."

Ministry is asking the visitor, "Are you new here? Yes? Well, welcome. How wonderful that you brought your two children. They're beautiful. And you drove that far to be here? Good for you. When the morning's over, I trust you'll feel it was worth all the effort you made to come!"

See, God's specialty is restoring broken lives. And as members of His family we should be good at that as well. Much of church life is about helping people solve their many problems—with Jesus as their new source of strength.

Ministry-oriented people are never satisfied with the kind of compliments an entertainer might want:

● You look great!

● Your music was marvelous. How did you hit those high notes?

● Your teaching is incredibly creative.

These are all more or less appearance issues. A ministry person wants to hear:

● That class helped me so much.

● Your song was like healing medicine to my soul.

● When you unfolded that Scripture the Lord really spoke to me.

Did you catch the difference?

I believe Christians want to be involved in churches with a ministry emphasis, not congregations that are appearance-oriented. So when compliments about church revolve around the looks of things, be aware of a possible problem.

● Your sanctuary is so gorgeous it takes my breath away.

● I'm pleased to report that as our suburb has grown so has our attendance.

● Our choir is incredibly skilled. In fact, they've made three recordings to date and have plans for a fourth.

Now that's in contrast to remarks like:

● This place is a sanctuary for me, a safe place to find healing.

● How loved I feel and how patient everyone has been with my slow progress in following Christ.

● This has to be the best family in the whole world. How privileged I am to be a member of it.

Churches that move ahead aren't immobilized by a perfectionistic mind-set. In fact, they anticipate mistakes, messes, and sins. You see, churches have to do with people. And people make mistakes—lots of them. If there's a way to mess up, sooner or later they'll discover it. People are also adept at sinning. Maybe you've noticed!

One way a church moves forward is by allowing its people to exercise their spiritual gifts. Scripture teaches that all believers have at least one such special skill, or God-given gift, to use in behalf of the body. The role of leadership involves helping people discover their gift—or more likely their gifts.

Sometimes church leaders are reluctant to set people free to use their gifts. They fear these individuals won't do their job in a way the leaders are comfortable with. Somebody might prefer a different style of music, or be too aggressive in evangelism, or teach something other than what's in the quarterly, or organize things in a new way. So, better keep tight controls. Make sure everything is done our way. Don't delegate a task unless we're absolutely sure this person can be trusted not to rock the boat.

And the church becomes paralyzed because it can't tolerate the possibility of somebody messing things up.

Another example: Often an individual church member doesn't respond excitedly and say, "Sure, I'll take on that responsibility!" Why? Perhaps it's because she's afraid she won't be able to do it perfectly. Maybe someone will criticize the finished product, or her report won't cover every possible objection, or the deadline might be missed, or the music will prove too difficult for the kids, or the committee members won't be able to come to agreement on her proposal. So the woman says, "I just don't think I have the time to take that on right now. I'm really sorry." But if she had been more honest her words would have been, "I'm terrified that I might not do it perfectly. I might make a mistake. So to be safe I'm saying no." And once again the church is unable to move ahead as it should.

CHURCH KITCHENS AND SANCTUARIES

Two specific rooms in the average church present particular problems in this regard. One is the kitchen.

Many congregational members have unusually strong feelings about the way the church kitchen should be cleaned up. They can get quite upset when dishes are put back in the wrong cupboards, and downright irate when parts of the coffeemaker are missing. "Look at this! Nothing's in the right drawer. Whoever was in charge of cleanup after last week's Father/Son Banquet ought to be shot!"

Visit the homes of everyone in the church and look at their kitchens! You'll quickly discover why each member has a totally different view about what the term "a clean kitchen" means. We're talking miles apart.

The easiest way to resolve this potentially nasty problem would be to eliminate the church kitchen altogether by transforming it into a library or a large supply room. But that would keep churches from moving forward because kitchens are really most useful resources. That is, if everyone can get used to it not being the perfect place they have in mind.

The other problem area, of course, is the sanctuary. Maybe you overheard the conversation the pastor had last week with Mary Beth about the banner she wanted to make for the wall by the organ.

You can almost hear what he's thinking, can't you? "We've never had a banner in the sanctuary before. If I let her make one, will it be any good? I mean, no great artist I can recall was ever named Mary Beth. Is she really gifted or does she just think she is? If her banner is awful, what do I do with it? You can't hang a banner in the men's room. Maybe I'd better call and tell her I've prayed about this and next year would be a better time. By then maybe that call from the church in Pleasant View will have come through for me."

Wait, Pastor! Don't touch that phone. Maybe Mary Beth will open up a whole new area of ministry in the church for artistic people. Take a chance. At least have her bring you a sketch of what she has in mind. Then you can get the opinion of others better qualified to judge her potential. But don't say no just because she hasn't yet produced a museum piece. Churches that move ahead are willing to risk making a mistake or two in the process of becoming what God has in mind for them.

One of the great ways to learn is what's called the trial and error method. Face it, we've all used it time and again. We did when we were young and we still do now. Eliminate trial and error and we miss out on many of the greatest lessons learned in life.

The church is too fearful of trial and error . . . too afraid something won't work perfectly on the first try.

I'm thinking about methodology, not doctrine. But then, maybe the church doesn't realize how much people learn even through the pain that comes as a result of sinning, even the sin of following false teaching.

James writes, "My brothers, if one of you should wander from the truth and someone should bring him back, remember this: Whoever turns a sinner from the error of his way will save him from death and cover over a multitude of sins" (James 5:19-20). Put your hand in the fire and you soon learn that's a foolish thing to do. That's also one of the ways we learn that sin isn't all the devil promises. Sin possesses an incredibly intense pain factor. So we become leery of it. And oh, the awful pain that over time affects a person who follows false doctrine.

But it's interesting to me that the Bible faces the fact that sin is common to individuals and common to the church. After a while we can more or less expect things to be that way. It doesn't surprise us. In the same chapter of James quoted above, "Therefore confess your sins to each other and pray for each other so that you may be healed" (v. 16). Apparently, James wasn't expecting everyone to be perfect, even within the family of God.

SIN FINDS IT WAY INTO THE CHURCH

So anticipate that sooner or later sin will find its way into the best of churches. Be prepared for it. Sin will affect relationships. It will try to worm its way into committee meetings, board meetings, staff meetings, even prayer meetings! But as the popular saying goes, what else is new? Sin doesn't take forward-moving churches by surprise, because they've never been immobilized by perfectionism.

Now, I realize I'm walking a fine line here. I'm not excusing sin. I'm just saying that sin shouldn't surprise church people. It shouldn't cause Christians to throw in the towel and say, "The fight's over. Because of the pounding we've taken, we can't answer the next bell!" Again, churches that move ahead anticipate mistakes, messes, and sins.

Before coming to The Chapel of the Air, I pastored an inner-city Chicago church for ten years. So I have a great concern for urban ministry.

Because of that, every year when we have pastors' conferences, to introduce our 50-Day Spiritual Adventure, I schedule some of the meetings to be held in inner-city churches. I still want to do what I can to bridge the gap between city and suburban congregations, and most of the time that difference means black and white.

Because pastors pay a healthy registration fee to participate, sometimes I'm a bit anxious as to how they'll respond in some of these settings. Many of them are used to attending conferences held in hotels like the Hyatt.

Several years ago we had a pastors' conference in a small black church in inner-city Syracuse. The auditorium was just large enough to hold the 125 attendees who came.

I remember one man from a quite well-to-do church thinking he had gotten the wrong address. This had to be a mistake. To him the neighborhood looked a mess. Then when he saw the Chapel of the Air sign out in front, he thought we had sinned against him.

He was noticeably upset. It didn't matter that the people of the church had worked overtime to make sure the building was the cleanest it had been in years. It meant nothing that the pastor had been the chef for former heavyweight boxing champion Larry Holmes, and the aroma from the kitchen in the basement was already letting us know the meal he would serve would be one of the best we'd ever had. It was a Thanksgiving, Christmas, and Easter feast all in one. The suburban pastor didn't notice that the people of the church who served as hosts and receptionists were incredibly friendly and efficient. This visiting pastor almost turned on his heels and left before hearing a word from us. The conference site obviously didn't match his concept of what a Chapel of the Air pastors' conference promised, and he let us know what he thought. I'm so glad he stuck it out.

At the end of the day this pastor apologized to many in the group. He thanked his hosts for a wonderful time and said he had learned more in those few hours than anyone could possibly imagine. He wasn't just talking about what the Chapel staff had taught him either. He said he was sorry for his initial reaction and hugged any number of his new friends.

As he left, I thought of how far he had come in so short a time, and I was thankful his preconceptions about the ideal conference hadn't robbed him of all this newfound joy. I hoped he'd also learned not to let future mistakes and messes and supposed sins block his progress as a church leader. I'd like to believe he changed that much.

The church isn't an exclusive club where appearances are crucial. A worship service is not like a theater experience that transports you to a world of illusion for an hour or two.

No, the church is a place where people who make a lot of mistakes can come and feel loved . . . and helped . . . and forgiven . . . and given hope to go out and do better next time.

Once we realize that, we'll all be a lot better off.

⌐ Galatians 6:1 has a flavor I'm trying to match here. "Brothers, if someone is caught in a sin [writes Paul], you who are spiritual should restore him gently." Do it kindly, tenderly.

You know what a gentle breeze is like. I'll bet you can almost feel it against your face right now. What a contrast to a harsh, howling wind. Paul says the restoration of someone who has sinned should be done in a gentle way, not in a fashion that's harsh or stormy. We should be much less concerned with appearance maintenance than with getting people's problems resolved with a tender touch.

"Watch yourself [Paul warns], or you also may be tempted. Carry each other's burdens, and in this way you will fulfill the Law of Christ. If anyone thinks he is something when he is nothing, he deceives himself" (vv. 1-3). Restated, don't pretend to be what you aren't.

First John 1:8 reads: "If we claim to be without sin, we deceive ourselves and the truth is not in us." Further (v. 10), "If we claim we have not sinned, we make Him [God] out to be a liar and His Word has no place in our lives." So all of us are not only flawed, we're sinners. We mess up before God and we often hurt others in the process. At one time or another all of us need that gentle, restorative touch.

So what about your church? Is it consistently adequate in helping believers mature spiritually? Is it consistently adequate in restoring those who mess up? Consistently adequate in terms of evangelism? Consistently adequate in its prayer life? Consistently adequate at praising God? Consistently adequate in waging spiritual warfare? Consistently adequate in its involvement in world missions?

If not, if there are major gaffes, if no one is growing much spiritually, if the congregation seems to bring God very little pleasure, if nobody's coming to Christ, if the church no longer even respects what He taught, then you need to look around for another place. You have good reason to start hopping!

But don't go church-hopping just because your church isn't perfect.

Lord,
I praise You for Your grace. You're not surprised that we sin,
and You graciously forgive us when we ask Your pardon. So we
don't have to struggle to hide our shortcomings or pretend we're
perfect. Your indwelling Spirit helps us in the process of growing
into Christ's likeness. Amen.

For Discussion and Reflection

1. How might perfectionism be a special problem for Christian families?

2. Are you comfortable with the term "consistently adequate," describing a reasonable standard for parents or leaders in healthy settings? Why or why not?

3. Are there ways you still buy into the illusion of a perfect church? If so, what is an example?

4. What experiences have you had with churches that are concerned more about appearances than true ministry?

5. Describe the difference between trying to do a good job and falling into the trap of perfectionism.

6. Is trial and error ever a valid way to learn spiritual lessons? When?

READINGS

Are you surprised that perfectionism is a characteristic of a dysfunctional family? It's rarely considered an unhealthy symptom, but it is a common source of many family problems, especially in Christian homes. After all, isn't the challenge of the Christian life to be perfect as God is perfect? Not really. We are called to live a life of excellence, which is attainable, not perfectionism, which is unattainable. Expecting perfect behavior from spouse or children, even in a Christian family, is living in a world of unreality.

A perfectionistic father conveys his standards and expectations through verbal rebukes and corrections, frowns, penetrating glances, smirks, etc., which continually imply, "It's not good enough." He lives and leads by oughts, shoulds and musts. These are "torture words" which elevate guilt and lower self-esteem. A father who constantly overfocuses on defects in a critical way erodes his child's self-image. The child begins to believe that he is hopelessly substandard, and he carries this poor self-image with him into adulthood.

Always Daddy's Girl, H. Norman Wright, Regal, pages 149–150.

■　■　■

Adult children of alcoholics tend to think in absolutes. Everything is always completely black or white, good or bad, right or wrong. And since we are never completely right, we are usually completely wrong. This mental characteristic is seen in adult children's abhorrence of process. Dan frequently asks when he will "get over this and be normal." His concept is like that of many other adult children of alcoholics: they are either "sick" or they are "well." Since they do not feel "well," and since they think in dichotomous absolutes, they fail to appreciate the small increments of positive change in their personal growth processes.

This thinking pattern may be behind the control orientation identified in most adult children of alcoholics. If you grew up in a chaotic family, you long to experience more order and control in your life. And if everything is either all under control or all out of control, you are going to work very hard to control *everything* and *everyone* in your life.

All-or-nothing thinking also leads to perfectionism, indecision, and self-hatred. The core of perfectionism is the belief that anything less than perfect is total failure. Perfectionism also fosters an illusion that you can control your world: "If only I can *be* perfect, find the perfect spouse, have perfect children, join the perfect church, and get the perfect job, my life will be under control and I will be happy." Alas, this thinking dooms its adherents to lives of guaranteed misery.

Adult children of alcoholics may experience the paralysis of perfectionism which leads to difficulty making decisions. They tend to be indecisive because they can never have perfect command of every fact needed to make perfect decisions. And these adults increasingly devalue and despise themselves as they are forced to confront the limitations of their humanity, namely imperfection. As children, they failed to perfectly control their alcoholic parent's drinking, and as adults they fail to attain their unrealistic and unreachable goal of personal perfection. In extreme cases, this self-hatred leads to suicide attempts and completions. In all cases, it contributes to depression and other disturbing emotions.

Counseling Adult Children of Alcoholics, Sandra D. Wilson, Word, pages 69–70.

■ ■ ■

Imagine a high-jumper in the Olympics. Every time they raise the bar, he clears it. Finally he jumps higher than all the rest and wins. But instead of standing on the center platform and receiving the prized gold medal, he raises the bar even higher. He tries several times, and falls with each attempt. Then he walks away dejected, feeling as if he lost the contest. Many perfectionists live this way. This sense of failure naturally produces frustration and anger against other people and often against God. As long as they live under the bondage of the performance-treadmill, they will be angry. Life will seem unfair and God will seem unjust. This will result in a range of negative feelings.

The hurts and humiliations perfectionists suffer keep their anxieties and anger churning. And not all of the anger is directed outward, for perfectionists live with a unique *combination of pride and low self-esteem*. They *always* suffer from a self-depreciation that *comes from fearful pride*. They are afraid others will discover the terrible gap between their *real selves* and their *fantasy selves* and then reject them. So they beat the public to the punch. *They reject themselves by putting themselves down before anyone else can. In this way their false pride in their superself is kept intact.*

We see this prideful self-rejection every day in perfectionistic Christians who cannot accept compliments without going out of their way to belittle their accomplishments. They must impress you with their humility and not let you catch them with their pride showing!

Freedom from the Performance Trap, David A. Seamands, Victor Books, pages 102–103.

■ ■ ■

Churches that have God's perspective function as "therapeutic communities." No one is surprised that Christians have serious problems; there are programs in place to help solve them.

Shame-based churches do not function as therapeutic communities because they believe that God expects a different kind of person to populate the pews. Instead of the bankrupt, the bound, the blind and the bruised, shame-based churches want to project the image of being filled with the prosperous, the prestigious, the pretty and the problem-free. They don't want broken people. They want perfect people.

Did you hear about the patient at Mt. Carmel Mercy Hospital in Detroit who was shot dead as he lay in his hospital bed recovering from a previous gunshot wound?

A hospital staff person said that the victim had been listed in fair condition prior to the [second] shooting and was looking forward to going home. Hospital patients and employees were stunned. A spokes-person said that nothing like this had happened in 50 years of the hospital's existence.

I'd say that that hospital (with only one shooting in fifty years) was a pretty safe place compared to some shame-based churches that regularly shoot their wounded members! Shooting the wounded makes sense if churches are supposed to be filled with perfect people. In such churches, problems are an intolerable embarrassment and must be denied, even if it means destroying bruised and broken believers in the process. . . .

What a distortion of God's purposes for His church! The body of Christ is meant to be a fellowship of sin-broken believers in the process of being restored to wholeness. The fact that you are not a perfect person or a totally transformed Christian does not make you "different-and-less-than." To some degree, *all* of us Christians struggle with the effects of past and present sin in our lives. Try to find a church that accepts this truth.

Released from Shame, Sandra D. Wilson, InterVarsity Press, pages 158–160.

■ ■ ■

Pastors must no longer teach just the biblical ideal of the healthy home, but must address with compassion the problems of the dysfunctional home. Does our traditional interpretation of submission hold true when substance/process addictions bring on sexual and physical abuse? What are we teaching that will minimize the risk of vulnerability to quick-fix mood-altering substances and processes? The temptations created by living in an addictive society and a dysfunctional home need desperately the healing touch of Christ through His Church. But often when hurting people turn to the Church what they find is an extension of the dysfunctional family.

Seeing unfortunate happenings, in the Church, the third institution actually contributing to addiction, does not suggest a lack of love for her. The Church is the Body for which Jesus poured out His life and blood. He watches over her with an eternal commitment and pours out upon those able to receive it, lavish manifestations of His grace and power. She is His only plan for spreading the Gospel to a lost world and the only suitable container for His generations of harvests. The Church will go on until His coming when she will glow in bridal attire and rise to meet her faithful Lord. The local church, the expression of Christ's Body in every place, is to be a healing home in which the sick and hurting can be restored to emotional and spiritual health.

All too often, however, churches are full of wounded people, the products of dysfunctional homes who themselves have never been healed and, therefore, reproduce after their kind emotionally dysfunctional and spiritually stunted members. Carrying their hidden rules into church, Christians create the same problems with communication and stable relationships. The unhealthy solutions they learned in the home are often applied to situations in the Body of Christ, resulting in broken fellowship and much hurt. Church-hopping becomes the norm as the dysfunctional person isolates himself and discards relationships with those who disappoint him, ever searching for the perfect church and the perfect pastor.

When Addictions Come to Church, Melinda Fish, Chosen Books, pages 39–41.

CHAPTER SEVEN

FROZEN FEELINGS

● Feelings. That's an area where some people are at a disadvantage. They aren't good at knowing what they're feeling.

Ask them what they learned at a lecture, ask them what they said in a recent conversation, ask them their opinion, and that's easy. But ask them what they're feeling and they're on shaky ground.

IDENTIFYING FEELINGS
Yet feelings play a big part in the life of healthy individuals and healthy families. So it's an advantage to be able to properly identify and express emotions.

A friend was going through some hard times with an adopted daughter, so their family went for counseling. "One thing I learned," he told me, "was that when she gets upset, I need to stop listening only to her words, and start noticing the feelings she's expressing as well. Before, I kept trying to *understand* her. That was so I could respond logically. Now I've learned to pick up on her emotions instead of just her words. Sometimes I say, 'I'm not sure I understand what you just said, but I sense you're trying to tell me you're extremely upset. Is that right?' "

I laughed—not *at* my friend, but *with* him. You see, I too am relatively new at this business of listening for messages

122

behind the words being used. That's because for a large part of my life I was tuned out emotionally. I wasn't aware of where others were coming from, and I didn't even understand my own feelings.

I was probably extreme in that regard. I didn't know when I was tired. I seldom paid attention to whether I was hot or cold. I wasn't in touch with what I liked or didn't like. If someone would ask me what was wrong, instead of saying, "I feel trapped with no way out of this situation," I'd reply, "I'm OK, why do you ask?"

Most of the time if someone accused me of expressing a negative emotion like anger or pride or frustration, I denied it. Was I stomping mad? No. Did I swear? Had my words stopped making sense because of my intense emotion? Never. What do you mean I was angry? You're accusing me of not acting the way a Christian should!

"You were emoting," my wife would tell me the next day. "It was as if you were sending out waves and waves of high voltage electricity. I don't understand how everybody can sense that except you."

Well, I wasn't in tune with my anger, my pain, my loneliness, my defensiveness, my fears, delights, moods, embarrassment, jealousies, whatever.

I functioned relatively well in the objective world of ideas and facts and words. But the more subjective realm of feeling was atrophying, shriveling up within me.

Thank God that in recent years the Lord has been doing a major healing in me for which I'm extremely grateful. One of the signs of health is that my feelings are coming back into play.

• When I go to church I often find myself filled with inexplicable joy.

• Tears come to my eyes when I'm emotionally wounded, or when I injure someone else.

• Now my body is able to get through to my brain when I need a rest.

• As I read the Bible I'm seeing how feelings are so much a part of the Scriptures.

Psalm 109:8-9 is an example. David is telling the Lord that a wicked man in leadership has spoken against him, has lied about David, and the attack was without cause. Listen to part of David's prayer. "May his days be few; may another take his place of leadership. May his children be fatherless and his wife a widow."

Ah, Lord, I'm thinking, *isn't that like asking You to kill this guy? Do You want me to teach people to pray like that?*

"May his children be wandering beggars; may they be driven from their ruined homes" (v. 10).

I wonder if this prayer isn't a bit extreme.

"May a creditor seize all he has" (v. 11).

Oh, my!

"May no one extend kindness to him or take pity on his fatherless children" (v. 12).

Lord, what if a new Christian reads this psalm? He could start praying some awful thing. This passage doesn't agree with what Jesus teaches about forgiveness.

"May his descendants be cut off, their names blotted out from the next generation" (v. 13).

The descendants aren't to blame for what this one guy did. My kids weren't responsible for my deeds.

What's that, Lord? Don't pay that much attention to his words? Catch the feelings David's expressing? I'll try.

"May the iniquity of his fathers be remembered before the Lord" (v. 14a).

Now David's going the other direction — backward. He's praying against this man's dad.

"May the sin of his mother never be blotted out" (v. 14b).

Lord, are You listening to this?

OK, OK, catch the feelings. David's telling You he's really upset about the lie this enemy told. I can see that.

"May their sins always remain before the Lord, that He may cut off the memory of them from the earth" (v. 15).

Wow, I'd say David's really off-base theologically, Lord.

You say that basically David's just telling You he feels trapped with no way out, and he desperately needs your help. And You would rather have him be honest with You about his feelings than to say "I'm OK, God, why did You ask?"

You say You're acquainted with another David who's been known to be that way? Yes, I understand.

God, I guess we're back to that course You're teaching me on feelings, aren't we?

FROZEN FEELINGS

Frozen feelings are often a trait of dysfunctional families. Certain members, or maybe all of them, are out of touch with their feelings. They're like the mother in Judith Guest's popular book *Ordinary People*. An upper-class suburban family is facing incredible emotional tensions. Most of these stem from the accidental drowning of one of the sons which occurred some time earlier. In the 1981 film version, now on video, Mary Tyler Moore plays the mom, a woman who goes about her daily living with an almost machine-line precision. She does everything "right," but she's cold and not very human. Her feelings are frozen. When I hear that term, her role is what pops into my mind.

Families with frozen feelings are usually uncomfortable around what they call "touchy feely" people.

People with frozen feelings don't experience the highs and lows of family life. They live in a limited middle range of emotion.

They put the kibosh on shouting and yelling. They say, "If we can't talk about these matters without getting all emotional, we'll just have to leave them alone."

They aren't much good at affirming one another. They have trouble saying things like, "You're a terrific son, and what a good job you did on the yard today."

Families with frozen feelings aren't very open when it comes to talking about their pain.

They don't cry very much either, even when they face the death of a loved one. But they're good at seeing that all the funeral details are taken care of.

What about members of church families? Do they sometimes have a problem with frozen feelings? Are they:

● leery of the "touchy feely" types?

- concerned about objective truth and suspicious of subjective ways of learning?
- highly cerebral, extremely logical, but kind of shriveled up feeling-wise?
- reluctant to openly express their thoughts and feelings in public gatherings?
- cautioning, "Let's talk about this without getting all emotional" whenever someone raises his or her voice?
- unskilled at telling a person, "I'm not sure what you said. But I sense you have strong feelings on this issue. I believe that for whatever the reason, you're against our congregation taking on another mortgage before the old one is paid off"?
- having trouble affirming people when they do a good job?
- likely to answer, "I'm not upset" when called by a fellow board member the morning following a highly charged late-night meeting several stormed out of?
- inclined to think that feelings like fear, anger, and disappointment are always unchristian?
- restricting church life to a small, middle range of emotions, and missing the highs and lows?
- embarrassed whenever someone cries or sobs?
- always making sure that above all else, their theology is right? (So don't preach a sermon on Psalm 109!)

HEALTHY FAMILIES AND FEELINGS

My premise is that healthy families (and healthy church families) learn how to properly identify and express their feelings. Their members can say, "I'm angry," or "I'm sad," or "I'm upset," or "I'm delighted," and having identified what they're feeling, "functional" families find appropriate ways to express their emotions.

When I'm trying to learn something new—whatever it might be—instruction guides usually don't help me much. I find they tend to be written by people who know so much about their field, they can't identify with the neophyte who's never put up dry wall, or operated a word processor, or explored the subject of codependent relationships.

When I'm learning about a new and confusing topic, what I really need is for someone to say, "Watch what I do. I'll demonstrate what's expected."

CHRIST AND FEELINGS
In this sense I've found the Christ of Scripture to be extremely helpful as a model of how to properly express feelings. The older I get, the more impressed I am with our young King.

I believe He's truly the Son of God because He rose from the dead. But I'm also convinced He's who He claimed to be because no mere human in His early thirties could be as wise and as emotionally healthy as Christ was. After all, I'm nudging 55 and I still have so much to learn in these areas.

Let's look at some accounts of Jesus' emotion-filled final week of life. I've chosen three quite different incidents. The first is found in Luke 19:28-44, which concerns His triumphal entry.

I remember the Chicago crowds welcoming home the Bears in 1985 after they won the Super Bowl. That scene was repeated when the Chicago Bulls won the National Basketball Association championship in 1991. This passage conjures up those same feelings of excitement as Christ approaches the Holy City to the acclaim of the cheering crowds. "When He came near the place where the road goes down the Mount of Olives, the whole crowd of disciples began joyfully to praise God in loud voices for all the miracles they had seen. . . . Some of the Pharisees in the crowd said to Jesus, 'Teacher, rebuke Your disciples!'

" 'I tell you,' He replied, 'if they keep quiet, the stones will cry out' " (vv. 37, 39-40).

Now He's almost to the sacred walls and suddenly everything changes. "As He approached Jerusalem and saw the city, He wept over it" (v. 41).

I don't think Jesus just sniffled a time or two. I believe His tears were obvious. In the Middle East when people weep, they really weep.

Our Lord saw Jerusalem's walls standing majestically before Him. If you've been there, you know how Jerusalem's walls do something to you. They're emotionally charged in some strange way. Now Jesus was looking up at them.

Andrew Hodges captures some of what happened at that moment in his book called *Jesus: An Interview across Time.* He pictures our Lord saying, "With all the shouting going on around me, I remember thinking, 'O Jerusalem, isn't eight hundred years of suffering enough? Since the days of David and Solomon, you have been constantly persecuted. Rulers have made war on you time and time again, destroying your families and taking your children captive. What's it going to take? Can't you hear the prophets? Even though you've ignored them before, listen to them now. You have another golden opportunity. This time it is a once-in-a-lifetime chance' " (New York: Bantam Books, 1988, p. 295).

In the very center of a wild celebration, here is a pain-filled and incredibly lonely moment for our Lord.

Personally, I'm glad Christ wept and that He explained why He did.

It wasn't because of self-pity. Primarily, He was showing compassion—compassion for spiritually slow people who should have been wiser, people who would pay a huge price for their ignorance and sin, people a lot like me and probably a lot like you. *Thank You for revealing what You were feeling, Lord. The crying, it meant You really care.*

The other day we had a luncheon for ten Chapel employees I had to let go because of the recession and a decrease in donations. Some of these people had been with us many years. The friendships were close. In the middle of my closing remarks I had to choke back tears. Later, one of the women being released said that when she saw the tears she knew I cared.

That was such a minor incident compared to the historic magnitude of this event Luke recorded. *But Jesus, when I see Your tears in this passage, I'm glad that frozen feelings didn't characterize You. That would have robbed me of knowing that even at Your time of greatest acclaim, You had tender thoughts about us, and You really cared.*

Ecclesiastes 3:1, 4, 8 reads, "There is a time for everything . . . a time to weep and a time to laugh . . . a time to love and a time to hate."

So by contrast let's look at Mark 11:12-17. This event takes place the day after the Triumphal Entry. In these verses Christ twice shows His anger. First He puts a curse on a fig tree because it doesn't have any fruit.

Then He drives the money changers from the temple. If ever there was a time the Jewish temple should have been marked by earnest praying, it was now. But again there was no appropriate fruit to show. The long-awaited Messiah had arrived and His Father's house of prayer for all nations had been made into a den of robbers.

At such a time what true king would do nothing?

If a President returned after a long absence and his staff had openly abused the White House, and he said nothing or did nothing, you would question whether he knew how a President should act.

What Jesus did here was appropriate. Yes, He was angry. But He didn't maul anyone. He just cleared out the offenders by force, said why He did it, and that was that.

Again, I'm glad Christ acted the way He did. To me it shows He knew who He was and also that He was incredibly brave. He laid down the gauntlet knowing full well that it would mean a fight to the death.

Another side of Christ's feelings is revealed in Mark 14:1-9. It's now only two days before the Passover. This is the account of the woman who anoints Jesus' head with very expensive perfume.

When the apostles react, Christ feels defensive. He says, "The poor you will always have with you, and you can help them any time you want. But you will not always have Me. She did what she could. She poured perfume on My body beforehand to prepare for My burial" (vv. 7-8).

This passage reveals that it's hard to reduce the showing of emotion to a simple list of instructions that will work for anyone at any time.

Yes, Jesus says, always be concerned about the poor. But don't use that as an excuse to overlook the massive inner struggle your leader is having to go through. Because he will carry the unbearable burden, it's appropriate to go to extremes to show you understand, that your heart is breaking too. Bless you, good sister.

So in this chapter I haven't tried to come up with instructions for when to cry and when not to. Anger is OK in this situation but not that one. Sometimes it might be all right to be defensive, but it's hard to say exactly when.

The simple truth is that Christ's emotions while He was on earth went far beyond the range often portrayed in the average Passion Play. In real life He didn't just move from one scene to another, delivering spiritual platitudes as if He were trying out for a job as an old-time radio announcer.

His feelings were not frozen. You get the impression they were very much as they should have been. As His mind had been "tuned" by His Father, so His emotions had been as well. God's people can look to His Son for an example of how to express feelings in a healthy fashion.

So yes, when someone in the church gets mad, this person could express it in a way that's not Christlike, if the anger gets out of hand. But it's also possible that by refusing not to acknowledge the emotion the individual is straying from Christ's example. Such a person needs to ask, *Why do I feel this way? How might Christ respond in my situation?*

When tears come, ask yourself, *Why am I crying?* Or *Why can't I cry, Lord, is my response appropriate?*

Were we defensive as a committee? Were our actions justified or not, Lord? Are we in tune with You or out of tune? And by the way, thank You for making us the way You have. What complex creatures we are. But we like it that way.

Lord,
I praise You for Your feelings. In the Scriptures we see You showing emotions that range from love and joy to disappointment and even anger. To be made in Your image is to have feelings. Help us learn to express our emotions appropriately. Amen.

For Discussion and Reflection

1. How often have you expressed anger to God the way David does in Psalm 109?

2. In Scripture, God is characterized by love, but also by jealousy, wrath, sadness, etc. How does that make you feel?

3. As you look back on your life, have you ever seen church family members who had a problem with frozen feelings?

4. What is an appropriate church setting for people to openly express their feelings? What is an inappropriate setting?

5. Why is it difficult to make a list of rules as to when various feelings are or are not appropriate to show?

6. What is a situation in which it would be proper to express feelings of anger? Feelings of pride? Feelings of fear?

READINGS

I do not believe that God has called us to be superhumans. One of the biggest mistakes we can make is to be misled into thinking that if we are Christian believers, we should never allow our emotions to get the better of us. It is wrong to think that we should always be in complete control of every feeling. This idea leads to inauthenticity—a sort of phoniness which ruins our witness and destroys our effectiveness in helping others. It also sets us up for developing mental and emotional problems.

I once knew a woman missionary who was one of the most controlled and disciplined persons I had ever met. Nothing could ruffle her. She was always calm, never angry, and seemed to be able to handle all the big blows that life could deal her without getting upset. On the surface she gave the impression that she was a saint, but there was something about her that made people afraid of her. Was she too perfect? Perhaps, but it was a "perfection" that hinted at inauthenticity. She couldn't really be trusted.

While she was admired by most of those who knew her and with whom she worked, her witness tended to produce guilt in others. It made them feel hopelessly inadequate in comparison with her. When her friends and acquaintances reflected on how they felt and then compared their reactions to hers, they felt hopeless failures. Rather than be attracted to her, they wanted to avoid her. She showed up their flaws! They never shared with her how they felt, nor could they ever go to her for counsel. What a sad situation!

Then one day she came to me for help. "Please don't tell anyone I have been to see you," was her opening remark, as she began to tell about how troubled she was by her emotions and how she had to work so hard at keeping her feelings under control. She dared not display her feelings for fear that she would be perceived to be a "poor witness" for her Lord. I assessed her to be on the verge of a serious breakdown. Yet to the very last, she was determined not to let anyone else see her vulnerabilities. Unfortunately, this determination, to a large extent, was responsible for her problem. She was in emotional trouble precisely because she was preventing herself from giving free expression to her feelings.

As I worked with her in psychotherapy, one of the strategies I used was to move her toward being more "authentic" and honest about herself. I encouraged her to share her emotional struggles with others. As a result, she found that she could better control them. The effect on her ministry was dramatic. She was now being perceived as more human, and her struggles and other experiences became sources of insight and encouragement to others. They modeled healthy spiritual disciplines, and she taught others how to deal with their emotional struggles more effectively.

I repeat: we are not superhumans. We do not have to be dominated and disturbed by our emotions. We also need not be so afraid that we avoid them. Emotions must be woven into our spiritual lives in such a way that they produce a harmonious and complementary pattern of wholeness. Our emotions are not in conflict with our spirituality. Emotions themselves are not sinful. They do not have to disturb our spiritual well-being but can be used to complement and enhance it.

Unlocking the Mystery of Your Emotions, Archibald D. Hart, Word, pages 2–4.

■ ■ ■

Feelings are as common as breathing, as useful as the utensils in my kitchen, as rich as Fort Knox, as varied as the flowers in gardens, as spectacular as fireworks on the Fourth, as annoying as a flat tire, as awful as an earthquake. What a shame so many Christians have colored them yellow-brownish-gray and stuffed them in storage. God built feelings into us for growth, maturity, fulfillment. They need fresh air. We think that opening the closet door is risky. We get alarmed because feelings seem hard to handle. We get caught in the "battered feelings" syndrome.

Why do Christians batter their feelings? Even if we come to the place where we're ready to listen to what's happening inside us, why do we have this grudge against feelings? One reason may be a response to our culture. When we see people "do their thing," follow the dictates of their feelings, we see them as contributing to society's problems. If feelings lead people into destructive activity, the less attention we give them the better.

Another reason we're wary of feelings is that we suspect they're unreliable. We find them fickle and flighty. They lift us up and let us down. Highs don't last and lows are painful. We think that growing spiritually is a matter of climbing steadily upward, getting better and better, and we can't rely on anything as unstable as feelings to get us to the top.

Then again there are the times of crisis when we move our bodies and minds to meet emergencies. Feelings seem immaterial. We behave well and we suppose it didn't take feelings to do it.

The main reason we can't look squarely at our feelings is that they help us see our real "self," and we don't like what we see. If we free our feelings to be felt, they just add to our age-old tendency to be disappointed with ourselves. So often they're "bad": anger, envy, suspicion, the emotions of temptation, the vague uneasiness that grips us from time to time. We've been told that Christians have been lifted up out of all that. If anyone knew what bad things are going on inside us, we would be found "unspiritual." The result is that we spend a great deal of energy keeping feelings in storage so we won't have to worry about what others think. We sit in self-judgment as well.

Feelings, Joan Jacobs, Tyndale House, pages 21–22.

■ ■ ■

One of the dysfunctional family's rules, usually unspoken, is "Don't feel." In one way or another, children are taught not to express their emotions. It is not uncommon, then, that as adults they find it difficult to acknowledge, identify or talk about feelings. Children who never hear their parents talk about feelings may grow up believing it is never appropriate to share emotions, or they may simply be unable to do so. As a child I never heard my father tell me that he loved me. For a long time after I was married, I found it impossible to say "I love you" to my wife.

Negative emotions are even harder for people in dysfunctional families to deal with. Anger in particular is a big issue for many adult children. In many respects, we have a lot to be angry about. We have often been victims of abuse or in some way have been deprived of healthy childhoods. But we don't know how to deal with anger, in mature, healthy ways. Most of us have grown up in environments which taught us that the best thing to do with feelings is to act like we're not feeling them.

Emotions are physiological energy; they eventually get expressed, one way or another. Anger turned inward is a deadly force, leading to physical symptoms like ulcers or emotional ones like depression. Anger also breeds resentments and bitterness, which slowly but surely dominate our character and turn us into sour, negative people. And even when we've done our best to stuff our anger under the rug, it leaks out the sides, manifesting itself in sarcasm and other unintentionally harmful behavior.

Some have learned to use anger as a shield. Other people walk around them on tiptoes, afraid of setting off a torrent of angry words. They have no idea what action or comment might touch a point of insecurity and set off the big guns. This kind of anger is abusive and keeps others from getting too close.

Strongest in the Broken Places, Dan Harrison, InterVarsity Press, pages 24–26.

■ ■ ■

During revival, emotions are expressed (who can be dry-eyed when bitter family relationships are dissolved?) but the meetings were free of emotionalism, that is, attempts to elicit emotional responses from the audience. Most of the observers were surprised to find the meetings quiet and subdued.

Flames of Freedom, Erwin W. Lutzer, Moody Press, page 161.

■ ■ ■

That afternoon when I encountered Jesus Christ, I was completely surprised by what I now know was the inrushing of the Holy Spirit. He came and put the risen King on His throne in my heart. He flooded me with the love of God and with irrepressible joy. I began jumping and shouting there in my little room.

There was no one about and I needed to tell someone, so I rushed out onto the road and hailed the first person I met, shouting, "Jesus has come my way! I'm forgiven!"

The person was a Christian woman, a church member, but perhaps she thought I was mocking, as usual, for she went off wagging her head.

I had to find someone else, so I ran to the church. God's people were still there and had been there ever since the morning service, because one after another had been finding Jesus that day. This was a common occurrence in Uganda in those days.

When I burst in, I excitedly told them my news and they took me into their arms, singing and rejoicing. Some laughed and some wept for joy. One after another embraced me with comforting words. Others did a kind of happy dance around me. One big man put me on his shoulder and walked around with me, not realizing that he was acting like the shepherd who said, "Rejoice with me, for I have found my sheep which was lost." My little sister and niece were there and I loved them. They had been expecting me.

One beautiful thing was that I was welcomed equally by the saints of the various tribes, and I now felt entirely different toward the people of other tribes than I ever had. I knew we were all one, and it was beautiful. The cross that rescued them had rescued me and the tribal barrier was gone.

When we all sat down, my tears were flowing fast, and so one of the brothers read from the New Testament the story of the sinful woman weeping at Jesus' feet.

I could picture that street woman after meeting with Jesus in the house of Simon the Pharisee. She must have rushed out of the house and begun telling everyone she met about her forgiveness. No doubt she found herself in the arms of Mary Magdalene and the other forgiven ones. I can hear her telling them all about it.

"I was miserable and lonely for so long and kept hearing about Jesus of Nazareth. So today when I saw Him going into the house of this Pharisee, I just followed Him in. I know Simon is judgmental and hard, but I *had* to see Jesus and nothing could keep me out.

"Jesus was reclining at table . . ." is perhaps the way she told them, "and they hadn't even been decent enough to wash His feet. I know, because I was holding them, and my tears came like a flood. I couldn't help weeping, because the burden was so great. I've hated myself and the life I've lived, and Jesus was so totally different from any man I ever knew before.

"When He turned and looked at me, I knew He understood me. His eyes were full of forgiving love that filled me with light and warmth. My heart began to vibrate because something wonderful was happening. No one accepts me, but He accepted me! I felt cleansed, covered, and put together.

"My tears kept coming and I was kissing His feet, wiping

them with my hair. I poured my perfumed oil on them. You can imagine how cold Simon looked—his eyes were like daggers. He was muttering ugly things to his friends against the Master. But Jesus was willing to take the blame and be misunderstood for me. Imagine that! The very words He said were: 'Your sins are forgiven. Your faith has saved you. Go in peace.' So now I am free and He is *my Lord* forever."

I had those same feelings and tried to speak them. All around me that Sunday evening my new brothers and sisters were listening to me and encouraging me and reading me the Scriptures. Each word was fresh and exciting, as though I had never heard it before. Over and over we sang the chorus:

> Yes, I'm washed
> In the blood,
> In the soul-cleansing blood
> Of the Lamb!

The Lamb! That was it. Suddenly the Old Testament account I had read in school fell into place. I could see an Israelite who knew he was a lawbreaker trudging toward the Tent of Meeting in the Sinai Desert with a lamb in his arms. I knew about white, spotless lambs because I had played with them when I herded my father's calves and sheep.

This man with the condemning heart would not have dared to go into the presence of God if he had not had with him this lamb, the provision God had ordained for the guilty. I could see him give it to the priest and then carefully lay his hand on its head.

He watches as the lamb's blood is spilled, knowing that God is graciously reckoning the lamb's death instead of his own. When it is done, the priest pronounces the man forgiven, and peace comes to his heart.

"I lay my sins on Jesus, the spotless Lamb of God," sang my new brothers and sister. Yes, God's Lamb was Jesus. What a costly sacrifice! How could the Father be willing to let His beloved Son leave Heaven to become the Lamb for my sin offering? But He did. And Jesus, hanging on the cross, was looking into my eyes, saying, "This death of Mine is reckoned as your death. Now you may have peace."

The new peace from Him was confirmed to me by the brothers and sisters who fully accepted me as one of the forgiven. They did for me the work of the priest at the door of the Tabernacle who assured the man with the lamb that now he was right with God.

One after another of God's family told me how Jesus had met him or her, and I was amazed at the variety of encounters, but always it was Love running to the rescue, to fill emptiness, to embrace loneliness, to wash away filth.

Later in the evening, some of the group accompanied me back to my house, and warmed it with singing. Someone brought in some food, but better yet was the spiritual nourishment of the conversation as they told me what Jesus was doing for them.

Revolutionary Love, Bishop Festo Kivengere, Christian Literature Crusade, pages 19–22.

CHAPTER EIGHT

THE INABILITY
TO CELEBRATE

● Bittersweet—that's what I'd call one of my favorite books, *Dinner at the Homesick Restaurant* by Anne Tyler. Talk about a dysfunctional family!

The Tulls live in Baltimore. The children, Jenny, Cody, and Ezra are fourteen, eleven, and nine when their salesman father, Beck, tells his wife, Pearl, he doesn't want to stay around. When he leaves she never says anything to the children, just pretends Dad is on the road again and that someday before long he'll be back home. But that doesn't happen.

As he grows older, Ezra, the gentle younger son, tries to live out his dream of a perfect family. Just once in his life he'd like all the Tulls to get together to celebrate a wonderful family meal. You know, the way it's supposed to be. But through the book this never happens.

When Ezra has the chance to take over a restaurant, he just knows this will provide the answer to his longtime wish. He even calls it the Homesick Restaurant.

It finally takes Mother Pearl's death to get the family together the way Ezra wants. But even then, for reasons I won't reveal, a stranger shows up at the meal, and the time together just doesn't work.

I'm sure the book was so popular because readers identified with the good and bad of the Tull family experiences.

And it seems Ezra Tull sensed intuitively, an important truth, that healthy families know how to make a celebration of special times together, such as meals.

CELEBRATION AND FOOD
Nowadays the whole fast food trend and mothers working outside the home militate against such thinking. Even so, celebration is one of the key characteristics included by Dolores Curran in her book *Traits of a Healthy Family* (New York: Ballantine Books, 1983). She states:

> These [healthy] families are very protective of the time allotted to the family dinner hour and often become angry if they're asked to infringe upon it for work or pleasure. A good number of respondents indicated that adults in the healthiest families they know refuse dinner business meetings as a matter of principle. They discourage their children from sports activities that presume upon the dinner hour as a condition for team participation. . . . And they never allow television to become part of the menu (p. 65).

Celebration in healthy families goes beyond sharing meals together. But food is often a part of the mixture.

I mention this because I'm aware of how often food is a part of the good memories people have of their experience in church families. As a matter of fact, is there any better food in town than what's served at a church potluck? In my lifetime I've been to a lot of them, and they're hard to beat!

Some families have little sense of celebration about them. They reason that birthdays and anniversaries and graduations are really like just any other day, and therefore they play them down.

They feel it's silly to make a big deal out of the Fourth of July or New Year's, Thanksgiving, or Memorial Day. Shouldn't we be thankful every day? Shouldn't we always be patriotic and appreciative of those who gave their lives for our freedom? In families like these the standard response to dinner invitations is, "We'll come over, but please, don't go to a lot of work for us, now." They have a low tolerance for festivity and ask, "Did you know that one of the reasons Rome fell was because she had so many holidays?" In contrast, healthy families understand the importance of celebration. They schedule special times and participate in them.

THE OLD TESTAMENT AND CELEBRATION

How fascinating that as far back as when the early books of the Old Testament were written the Lord established times of celebration for His people. The weekly Sabbath implied that men and women were more than workers, they were also worshipers. The Sabbath was to be a special time for both the individual family and the family of God.

Yes, the Sabbath is like every other day, and no, it's not like any other day. It's the pinnacle of the week. For devout Jews, Sabbath is so wonderful they need three days to mentally get ready for it. Then they are to enjoy it to the fullest. The next three days are necessary for the people to come down off the Sabbath high. Then the cycle of celebration begins all over again.

Three days to get ready, Sabbath the high point of the week, then three more days to reflect on the wonder of this great gift from God. How much Christians miss out on if Sunday is little more than "the one morning we go to church each week." When our culture changed its thinking about Sunday being special, it gave away a great national treasure.

Besides the Sabbath, God also established other special times of celebration for His Jewish people throughout the year. Each had its unique emphasis. For example, the Feast of Passover was different from the Feast of Pentecost. The Festival of Booths had a different feel to it, as did the awesome Day of Atonement. The Hebrew word *rosh* means "head" or "beginning." *Hashanah* is "the year." *Rosh Hashanah* is only mentioned once in the New Testament. The more common biblical name for this festival is the Feast of Trumpets. This feast celebrates a time of new beginnings with the Lord.

God instructed that once every fifty years the Jews would experience the marvelous Year of Jubilee. At this time Hebrew slaves would gain their freedom and all lands were to be returned to their original family owners. Who can conceive of the celebrating that was intended for that time?

Would the same God who established these times for His Old Testament people frown on a New Testament church that sets aside Holy Week to relive His Son's Passion? I don't understand Christians whose routine is always the same, whether it's Good Friday or Easter Sunday. That's like not knowing the difference between a funeral and a victory celebration.

Yes, the celebration of Christmas has become commercialized throughout North America. But that doesn't mean I can't love the carols and candles and generous gift-giving, and relive the wonder of the angels' proclamation, "For unto you is born this day in the city of David a Savior, which is Christ the Lord."

CELEBRATION AND THE FAMILY OF FAITH
Churches need to have a healthy respect for celebration and what it does for the family of faith.

One of my most cherished memories is of an Easter service in the middle 1970s at the church I was then pastoring in the heart of Chicago. I was to preach about the women who went to Christ's tomb and found it empty. Months earlier members of the congregation had started to put together the parts of the service.

A series of slides had been taken of two women in the congregation. These slides showed them getting up early in the morning. The women were obviously distraught. They ate a quick breakfast, got cleaned up, and took public transportation to a cemetery across the city. A short film was made of the same sequence with the same two women, same apartment, same clothes, and same cemetery.

That Easter Sunday as my message was coming to a close this media presentation began. First one slide, then another, then several all at once. As I finished the sermon most of the wall behind me was filled with changing shots telling the wordless story. Then in the middle section of the wall, the still shot dissolved into a moving picture. It was the film presentation showing the same two women from our church family living out the discovery of the Resurrection in our Chicago setting.

As they found the grave empty, the camera slowly zoomed out so that the entire cemetery could be seen with all its many grave stones. But one plot was broken open, and what now appeared to be two small figures were running excitedly to the cemetery entrance to go and tell their friends the good news. As the film was ending, the same two women in the same clothes came running from the back of the auditorium to the front and whispered in my ear, "He's risen, Christ is risen indeed. Pass it on!"

I immediately shared quietly with my staff on the platform. Then with the two women we went to people at various points in the congregation and one at a time we whispered, "He's risen, Christ is risen indeed. Pass it on." And the news rolled like a wave across that Easter morning crowd.

"This is truly news to celebrate," we told the worshipers. Then from the side rooms women wheeled out carts and carts of Middle Eastern food, figs, and grapes and cheeses and homemade breads and juice and wine. And right on the spot that Easter Sunday in church we shared our feelings about what this great victory meant to us, and we ate together as we celebrated this most wonderful of mornings.

It was a marvelous time. We didn't just use the word *celebrate*, we actually did it! And it felt so good. It became a memory I'll always treasure. We understood the importance of the celebration of this event, we planned for it, and we participated in it.

REVIEW

Let's review what we have been learning about traits of healthy families.

Knowing how something works enables you to fix it when it breaks down. That's true even of dysfunctional families.

I hope these chapters about the differences between dysfunctional and healthy families have proved to be of value. I know in my own experience I've found it extremely beneficial to have a standard to go by.

We have learned that:

1. In dysfunctional families love is given on the basis of performance. "Please me and you'll earn my love." In healthy families love doesn't have strings attached. It's unconditional.

2. A pattern of blaming and shaming marks dysfunctional families. In healthy families people don't point a finger at someone and say, "It's all your fault. You can't do *anything* right." Instead they ask, "What can I do to make this situation better?"

3. Unhealthy comparisons and competition mark families that don't function as they should. By contrast, in a properly functioning family, each person is valued for the unique individual he or she is.

4. Denial and delusion also are characteristics of a dysfunctional family. Whether it's laziness, drinking, or working all the time, the guilty party says, "I don't have a problem." Honesty is the hallmark in healthy families: "Yes, that's a problem I have, and it has to be dealt with."

5. The dysfunctional trait of compulsive/addictive behavior can keep unhealthy families from knowing freedom from such bondage.

6. Perfectionism and the subsequent need to impress — those are unhealthy traits. They stand in contrast to a family expecting mistakes and allowing room for them. Functional families seek to be consistently adequate, not perfect.

7. Frozen feelings characterize dysfunctional families, while healthy families are good at expressing their emotions.

8. Healthy families also enjoy times of celebration. Dysfunctional families experience difficulty having a good time.

There are more family dysfunctions than the eight I focused on.

● Dysfunctional families have rigid rules, rigid beliefs, rigid lifestyles. Healthy families demonstrate greater flexibility.

● There's an idealization of parents in dysfunctional families. In healthy families older children appraise their parents more realistically.

• Giving double messages as contrasted to giving consistent messages—that's another unhealthy trait.

• In dysfunctional families parents alternate between punishing their children and being permissive. There's consistent discipline in healthy homes.

My point in this book is that dysfunctional families need "change agents" who catch a vision of what could be and pray for God's help to make their dream a reality. With a family member's new knowledge of what's healthy comes a fierce determination not to perpetuate the same problems generation after generation. If at the start a family member has to go it alone without the support of the rest of the family, that's all right.

In his excellent book *Generation to Generation* (The Guilford Press, 1985), Rabbi Edwin Friedman writes:

> Were marital counseling always dependent on both parties attending, as many troubled spouses unfortunately believe, the less motivated partner could consistently sabotage progress by merely refusing to work on the relationship. It is often possible, however, to bring change to a relationship by "coaching" the motivated partner alone (pp. 78–79).

So bless all those determined souls who declare, "Even if I'm the only one in the family to pursue health, so be it. I'll do it anyway!"

Along with discussing dysfunctional family traits, in this book I've introduced the somewhat new idea that church families often demonstrate the same dysfunctions. That becomes obvious as you take the time to look at these characteristics one at a time, as we've done.

HEALING DYSFUNCTIONAL CHURCH FAMILIES

I suppose one could almost expect a church family to be the sum of its many parts. But if a congregation can be affected by the dysfunctions of its families, it can also benefit when those families begin to know healing.

This is what happens in Dr. Oliver Sacks' remarkable book *Awakenings*. In it he tells the true story of a hospital family that witnessed two miracles.

In 1969, a number of hopeless post-encephalitic patients in a small hospital in a New York suburb were given the drug L Dopa. In the film based on the book, Robert DeNiro plays the part of Leonard, one of these patients. In the book he's described as "in his forty-sixth year, completely speechless and completely without voluntary motion except for minute movements of the right hand. With these he could spell out messages on a small letter board—this had been his only mode of communication for fifteen years . . ." (Harper Perennial, a Division of Harper Collins Publishers. Copyright 1973, 1976, 1982, 1983, 1987, 1990, p. 203).

Early in the film we see Leonard with his mouth hanging open, his head torqued to one side, his hands curled in a grotesque manner. Hospitalized since his youth, Leonard is given large amounts of L Dopa by his doctor, played by Robin Williams. And Leonard "awakens."

After the drug therapy, he walks and talks much like a healthy human being. Sacks writes, "He was like a man who had awoken from a nightmare of a serious illness, or a man released from entombment or prison, who is suddenly intoxicated with the sense and beauty of everything round him" (p. 200).

The change is so amazing that the hospital staff collects enough money to administer the same massive and costly doses of L Dopa to a large number of similar patients. And then, all of a sudden, the awakening gives way to several awakenings as one by one these people become markedly improved and almost "normal," each manifesting a unique and delightful personality.

But something unforeseen is happening. Leonard is beginning to show decided side effects. They're sad to behold— violent ticks and jerks that rack his body. The doctors begin to realize that the awakening was just for a short period of time. First Leonard, and then all the others, will soon go back to their former state.

So the story is wonderful and also terribly sad. But then a second miracle occurs.

Before the awakenings, the staff of the hospital had viewed these pitiful people as just a part of their job ... someone to feed or to humor or to clean up again and again. Now the patients had become to the staff, unique individuals trapped by a terrible disease in the prison of their own bodies.

Through this experience the hospital staff came to understand more fully that these patients must be treated with dignity and love. In the months ahead, the staff would read to them, comb their hair, and go the extra mile to make sure they were as comfortable as possible. The film ends by saying that indeed the second miracle may have been more remarkable than the first.

So in this true story we see individual healings, but we also see a major corporate healing.

As I finish this short book I pray for the many Leonards whose lives have been so painful, damaged as youths in dysfunctional homes for which they were hardly responsible. I want to see them awakened from the awful prison that has kept them from being the people God intended. And I want their individual miracle stories to be without side effects or relapses. I believe that's possible because our Great Physician has a miracle touch.

In church after church, I also want each individual awakening to result in awakenings (plural) as one life touches another and many, intoxicated by the Spirit, sense the beauty of all that's going on around them.

I also pray there will be a great corporate change. I want the church to realize that institutions thought of as places of healing can sometimes end up treating wounded people as though they were little more than part of a job routine that someone has to do for the hopeless and the helpless.

But this is poverty thinking compared to what the church should be. In the mind of the Creator we were intended to be the marvelous family of God. We are brothers and sisters who have come into our relationship because of the common blood of Christ. This knowledge is what gives us confidence to truly be our Lord's new body in this present world, "the fullness of Him who fills everything in every way" (Eph. 1:23).

Do you see how wonderful this is? Do you understand that we are the best family in the whole world? Do you catch the vision of what could be *in your life* as you become whole, and *in our corporate life* when wholeness marks the church?

Do you comprehend that He is able to do "immeasurably more than all we ask or imagine, according to His power that is at work within us"? (3:20) His power is in us as individuals yes, but far more so in us as His new family. Notice Paul's words: "To Him be glory *in the church* and in Christ Jesus throughout all generations, forever and ever! Amen" (v. 21, italics added).

Lord,
I praise You for Your appreciation for celebration. You commanded Old Testament Israel to set aside feast days to celebrate Your presence. We delight in the way the seasons of the year offer You their varied praise. Each Sunday we go to church knowing that we will be honored by Your presence. You are worthy of our exultation. Amen.

For Discussion and Reflection

1. What is dysfunctional about individual or church families not being able to celebrate? Isn't this just a matter of personal preference?

2. When family meal times aren't protected, what is lost?

3. Can the way we observe Sunday/Sabbath become legalistic? If so, how? In what ways might our culture have drifted too far in the other direction?

4. What days or seasons of the church year are very special to you, and why?

5. Describe how you can be a positive "change agent" in your family.

6. What would be involved in your assuming a "change agent" role in your church?

READINGS

Some families ignore playtime for a variety of reasons; they develop an attitude that fun is peer-oriented and individualistic; their schedules are so full that family fun-time gets squeezed out; they lack spontaneity and come to believe that family recreation requires planning, equipment, and money, which may be in short supply; or they rely upon television as their sole recreational activity. Other families defer fun together until their annual vacation. Finally, and sadly, some families simply do not enjoy one another.

Playing together as a family sounds almost too simple, but it is a major factor in living with stress in the modern family. Many families spend a great deal of time together in child-related activities like league sports and scouting, but they don't play together as a family. I found that the families with the most ability to deal with everyday family tension are those who recognize the need to temper work and activities with shared play. "When tempers get short and tensions get high because we are so busy and pressured for time, we know we need to stop and have some fun," said a father.

Stress and the Healthy Family, Delores Curran, Winston Press, page 184.

■　■　■

The rhythm of the sacred with its holy anticipation—what a contrast to the typical Mains' family Sunday morning scenario in which the children invariably lost a dress shoe, or couldn't find their church school lessons; where someone would say the wrong word in the wrong tone and there would be an angry flare-up, and we would sit in wooden silence in the car waiting for the stirred emotions to settle so we could get over being mad in time to worship the Lord in the beauties of holiness.

I used to think this Sunday morning commotion ("Mo-om! Randy won't let me in the bathroom." BANG! BANG! "Hurry up! I gotta get in there!") was due to the fact that we were a ministerial family and some unbidden demonic force attempted to steal our good intents toward adoration. ("Who took my comb?" "Someone didn't put the milk back in the refrigerator last night!")

I used to think it was all my problem—I was a nice woman but a bad manager; and my awkwardness in running a household showed most on Sunday morning. ("Mo-om, I can't find any good stockings!" "You know I *hate* [those pants, that dress, this shirt, etc.]" I even identified with Martha in the Scripture story where Christ comes to visit the home of Lazarus and his two sisters. ("Mo-om, I don't wanna go to church today. I think I'm sick.") I knew what it meant to live with a Mary, except that my Mary was my husband.

I would hustle and bustle, find the missing shoe, iron the shirt that had been neglected the night before, throw the wet clothes into the dryer, set the table for ten for Sunday dinner, prepare a simple meal for guests, go over the last-minute preparations for our interracial Christian Education Center plans, then finally get myself dressed after a most inadequate catch-as-catch-can family breakfast. David would emerge from his study, holiness sitting on his brow, anointed to present the Word of the Lord to our congregation, oozing peace and equanimity. Oh yes, I knew how Martha felt when Mary sat at the feet of Jesus.

But then I discovered that many Christian families (not just those of us in pastoral ministry) had the same struggles.

Sunday morning, leaving for church, was often the worst time in their week.

As a couple, David and I vowed to work together to restore our observance of the Lord's Day, to seek to make Sunday the best day of the week, the high point, to struggle to establish this rhythm of the sacred in our lives as individuals and in our lives as a family. We wanted Sunday to become the joyful focal point of our weekly lives.

Now it's important to underline the word joyful. We did not want to slip back into an old legalism, that grim old joyless observance of the Lord's Day with its killing *can'ts* and *don'ts* and *won'ts* and *shall nots*. That attitude has done as much to create a dread of worship as anything I know. It was against this kind of legalism Christ had to continually speak. In three of the Gospels His words of reminder and rebuke are recorded, "The Sabbath was made for man, not man for the Sabbath." I wanted the kind of celebration in our family hearts that I read about in Isaiah and Deuteronomy:

> "If you . . . call the Sabbath a *delight* . . . if you honor it, not going your own ways . . . then you shall take delight in the Lord . . ." (Isaiah 58:13-14). "You shall *rejoice* in your feasts, you and your son and your daughter" (Deuteronomy 16:14).

Making Sunday Special, Karen Burton Mains, Word, pages 21–23.

■ ■ ■

On October 26 I witnessed the unrivaled joy of these people. It was Simhat Torah, the happiest of Jewish Holy Days, when the reading of the books of the law is completed for the year in the synagogue and Genesis is begun over again. I went to the Wailing Wall in the morning and found there the same throngs of black-clad Jews that I had seen before, bobbing and chanting in front of the stones, but here also were wildly shouting groups of men — well over a thousand of them — parading the huge parchment scrolls which had been brought forth from their synagogues. They put their hands on one another's shoulders and danced in a circle, shouting the praises of the Book, singing songs about the rebuilding of the Temple and the redemption of Jerusalem. Frequently I caught the words "Yerushalayim," "Israel," *"simhat"* (which I learned means "happy"), and *"adonai,"* the substitute for the ineffable name of God.

At the foot of the Wall, groups of men gathered with a prayer shawl held above them like a roof. This, I learned at last (for although the crowd was made up almost entirely of Jews, one after another told me he knew no more about what was happening than I did—I would have to ask a rabbi), was for the blessing of the scrolls. They would bring their scrolls —some were covered with large, elaborately filigreed silver cylinders, others with embroidered velvet sheaths, some topped by gold or silver crowns—and begin their own dance, weaving and circling among the others, eyes closed or lifted to heaven, bodies jerking and swaying with ecstasy, voices raised in lusty hymns. There were several oriental Jewish women sitting on a pile of rubble at one side, keening in the piercing, Arab ululation of joy or sorrow. When the men drew near with a scroll these women rocked with ecstasy, throwing kisses toward the sacred book, with tears streaming down their dark cheeks. Now and then I caught the word *"aleluyah"* from their shrieks. The dancing men paused at intervals to embrace the scrolls, to kiss them and clasp them in their arms, lifting them high as a young and strong lover might do with the woman he loved, while the other men increased their shouts and some of them waved flags. There were children riding on the shoulders of their fathers, laughing with the excitement of it all, bouncing high and victorious above the crowd.

Not much emphasis was ever placed on plain human happiness in my religious training. Our gatherings were careful and quiet and controlled. The "joy of the Lord" was to us a deep, serious thing not connected with celebrating in any way, let alone with dancing, and to find myself confronted with this wild abandon and told that it was the celebration of the written Word gave me pause. Deuteronomy 12 speaks of the Jews living in the land which God gives them, destroying the places of worship belonging to strange deities and making sacrifices to the Lord God, "happy before the Lord in all your undertakings." Clearly the Jews had something here that the rest of us had missed.

Furnace of the Lord, Elisabeth Elliot, Doubleday, pages 89–90.

■   ■   ■

From the beginning the Christian community expressed its faith through the arts. From the Roman catacombs where Christians met secretly to the great medieval cathedrals we find artistic offerings to God. The musical, dramatic, and visual arts played a significant role in the church's life and worship just as they served as effective means for education and catechesis. During the 9th and 10th centuries the liturgy of the church became increasingly dramatic; symbolic gestures, dialogical responses, and antiphones interspersed with anthems and hymns transformed the liturgy into a community drama and dance using all the senses for the worship of God and the nurture of humans. During the 11th century the churches erected in their naves scenes to be used in the dramatization of the Christian story from creation to the last judgment. Through pantomime and tableau the Scriptures were brought to life. By the 15th century, the average person was heir to a vital musical and dramatic and poetic tradition. In an age of illiteracy, the arts transmitted the Christian faith. Throughout the Middle Ages and much of the Renaissance, Western art was explicitly Christian in content and style. However, the age of reason combined with the reformation estranged the church and the arts. The artist sought liberation from the restraints of the church and the church turned its back on the artists. By the 18th century the divorce was all but complete. While society has never been without great religious art, their works typically have been restricted to galleries and museums. Today, church architecture is generally unimaginative. Few great paintings or pieces of sculpture adorn the church. Prints of sentimental pictures of Jesus and trivial pieces of music combine to further alienate the artist from the church. Drama is restricted to the children's Christmas pageant and dance is all but non-existent. Liturgy is typically a non-participatory event in which few of the senses are stimulated. The verbal and the intellect dominate liturgy and education. It is because of our overreliance on reason and neglect of feelings that Denise Levertov, the poet, suggests that the poet is in a peculiar way the believer today and the theologian and preachers the skeptics. Perhaps, however, that explains why attendance at music concerts, art museums, dance festivals and plays more significantly increased while church attendance has not.

Nevertheless, all this is changing.

"What Has Zion to Do with Bohemia," John H. Westerhoff, III, in *The Journal of Religious Education*, vol. 76, no. 1, Jan.–Feb. 1981, pages 11–12.